PassKey
Learning Systems

EA Review: Part 3
Single Course Workbook

Three Complete
IRS Enrolled Agent Practice Exams

Representation

May 1, 2023-February 29, 2024
Testing Cycle

Joel Busch, CPA, JD
Christy Pinheiro, EA, ABA®
Thomas A. Gorczynski, EA, USTCP

Executive Editor: Joel Busch, CPA, JD

PassKey Learning Systems EA Review Part 3 Workbook: Three Complete IRS Enrolled Agent Practice Exams: Representation (May 1, 2023-February 29, 2024 Testing Cycle)

ISBN 13: 978-1-935664-91-8

First Printing. April 15, 2023.

PassKey EA Review® is a U.S. Registered Trademark

Cover photography licensed with permission. Cover image ©Steve Allen, Dreamstime.com.

PassKey EA Review®, PassKey Learning Systems® are U.S. Registered Trademarks.

Official website**: *www.PassKeyOnline.com***

This workbook is designed for exam candidates who will take their EA exams in the *May 1, 2023-February 29, 2024* testing cycle.

Note: Prometric will NOT TEST on any legislation or court decisions passed after December 31, 2022. For exams taken between May 1, 2023-February 29, 2024, all references on the examination are to the Internal Revenue Code, forms and publications, as amended through December 31, 2022. Also, unless otherwise stated, all questions relate to the calendar year 2022. Questions that contain the term 'current tax year' refer to the calendar year 2022.

This page intentionally left blank.

Table of Contents

This page intentionally left blank.

Recent Praise for the PassKey EA Review Series

(Real customers, real names, public testimonials)

Perfect review book!
A. Mietzner
This EA review is great! It goes into detail. Explains why. When you do the practice test, it actually details the answer for learning and retaining! Definitely recommend!

Fantastic textbooks and video resources.
Vino Joseph Philip
Comprehensive and accurate video lessons are available online, and testing is also available for each course. I passed all three exams on the first attempt after using Passkey's resources.

Passed on the first attempt!
William Collins
I passed the first time with the Part 2 [textbook] for the EA SEE 2 exam. I also used the Part 1 textbook and passed that EA exam on the first try as well. Great resources!

I highly recommend these materials
Tosha H. Knelangeon
Using only the [PassKey] study guide and the workbook, I passed all three EA exams on my first try. I highly recommend these materials. As long as you put in the time to read and study all the information provided, you should be well-prepared.

I passed on the first try.
Jake Bavaro
I recently passed the first part of the EA exam using just the textbook and a separate practice test workbook. The textbook is very easy to read and understand. Although I have a background in accounting and tax, someone with little or no knowledge of either should be able to grasp all of the various topics covered in the book. I really do believe that it is a superior preparation resource.

I passed all three parts the first time taking them.
Sheryl Reinecke
I passed all three parts the first time. I read each chapter and the review quiz at the end of each chapter. Before taking the real exam, I did the practice exams in the additional workbook. I feel the material adequately prepared me for success in passing the exam.

Outstanding Material!
E. De La Garza
If you're looking to pass the EA exam with minimal expense, I recommend the PassKey system.

You can pass.
Vishnu Kali Osirion
I really rushed studying for this section. These authors make tax law relevant to your day-to-day experiences and understandable. You can pass the exam with just this as a resource. I do recommend purchasing the workbook as well, just for question exposure. The questions in the book and in the workbook are pretty indicative of what's on the exam. This is a must-buy. Cheers.

Absolute Best Purchase
Sharlene D.
This book was definitely worth the purchase. The layout was great, especially the examples! Reading the book from front to back allowed me to pass [Part 2]. I also recommend purchasing the workbook or subscribing to the material on their website for this section.

Excellent explanations!
Janet Briggs
The best thing about these books is that each answer has a comprehensive explanation about why the answer is correct. I passed all three EA exams on the first attempt.

PassKey was the only study aid that I used
Stephen J Woodard, CFP, CLU, ChFC
The [PassKey] guides were an invaluable resource. They were concise and covered the subject matter succinctly with spot-on end-of-chapter questions that were very similar to what I encountered on the exams.

Amazing!
Sopio Svanishvilion
PassKey helped me pass all three parts of the Enrolled Agent exam. They are a "must-have" if you want to pass your EA exams.

I passed all three with Passkey.
Swathi B.R.
I went through the online membership, read the whole book, solved all the questions, and passed the EA exam on my first attempt. For all three [parts], I referred to Passkey EA Review. Wonderful books.

Passed all 3 Parts!
Kowani Collins
Thank you so much for providing this resource! I have passed all 3 parts of the SEE exam. PassKey allowed me to study on my own time and take the exam with confidence. Thank you for providing such thorough and easy-to-follow resources!

Introduction

This PassKey EA Review Representation Workbook is designed to accompany the PassKey EA Review study guide for Representation, which presents a comprehensive overview of the material you must learn to pass Part 3 of the IRS Special Enrollment Exam (SEE), commonly called the EA exam. This workbook features three complete enrolled agent practice exams, specifically created for the EA exam cycle that runs from **May 1, 2023-February 29, 2024**.

Each sample exam has 100 questions, similar to the ones you will encounter when you take your actual exam. These test questions are all unique and not found in the PassKey study guides. This is intentional, so EA candidates can have a more true-to-life test-taking experience when they go through the workbook questions.

Any EA exam candidate will benefit from the exam questions and detailed answers in this workbook. We suggest that you use it as a study tool to prepare for the exam in a realistic setting. Set aside an uninterrupted block of time and test yourself, just as you would if you were actually taking the EA exam at a testing center.

Score yourself at the end, and then review the answers carefully. Unlike the Prometric exam, you will have a complete, clear answer for each question. If you miss a question, you will know why. Use this workbook to uncover your weak points and concentrate on improving in those areas. You should answer at least 80% of the questions correctly. Any score below 80% means you need to study more.

All of the questions in the workbook are based on **2022 tax law**, which corresponds with the current EA exam cycle. If you have any questions about the actual exam or if you want to sign up for it, go directly to the Prometric website at *www.prometric.com/IRS*. If you would like to find out more about the PassKey EA Review study program and other learning products by PassKey Publications, visit our website at *www.passkeyonline.com*.

Successfully passing the EA exam can launch you into a fulfilling and lucrative new career. The exam requires intense preparation and diligence, but with the help of PassKey's EA Review, you will have the tools you need to learn how to become an enrolled agent.

As the authors of the PassKey EA Review, we wish you much success!

This page intentionally left blank.

Essential Tax Law Updates for Representation

Here is a quick summary of some of the essential tax figures for the enrolled agent exam cycle that runs from May 1, 2023-February 29, 2024.

Study Note: Congress may enact additional legislation that will affect taxpayers after this book goes to print. Prometric will NOT TEST on any legislation or court decisions passed after December 31, 2022. For exams taken between May 1, 2023-February 29, 2024, all references on the examination are to the Internal Revenue Code, forms and publications, as amended through December 31, 2022.

Important Legislation for the 2022 Tax Year:

- The ***Inflation Reduction Act of 2022*** was signed into law on August 16, 2022. The bill includes dozens of expanded or extended tax credits and additional funding for the IRS.

- The ***SECURE Act 2.0*** was signed into law on December 29, 2022, as part of the *Consolidated Appropriations Act of 2023.* This bill added more than ninety new retirement plan provisions that affect individuals and businesses. Most of these provisions do not go into effect until 2023, but there are some provisions that are retroactive.

Due Date: Taxpayers will have until Tuesday, April 18, 2023 to file their 2022 return because the Emancipation Day holiday in Washington, D.C. falls on Sunday, April 16, 2023 and will be celebrated on Monday, April 17, 2023. The extended deadline is October 16, 2023, because October 15 falls on a Sunday in 2023.

FBAR penalties: For the purposes of the "non-willful" civil penalty mentioned directly above, on February 28, 2023, in a 5-4 decision, the United States Supreme Court ruled that this penalty applies per FBAR report - not for each reportable foreign account. Therefore, even if an individual has multiple reportable foreign bank accounts with a "non-willful" FBAR violation, only one civil penalty can be imposed on the taxpayer for the year. Prior to this decision, there was a split in the lower courts about whether the non-willful civil penalty could be imposed per FBAR report or for each reportable foreign account.

Passport Revocation threshold: The IRS can certify a taxpayer has "seriously delinquent tax debt," which can lead to the denial and/or revocation of a taxpayer's passport. The threshold in 2022 is $55,000, which includes penalties and interest.

Late filing penalties: If an individual taxpayer files their return more than 60 days after the due date, or extended due date, the minimum penalty is the smaller of $450 (for 2022) or 100% of the unpaid tax.

Penalty relief for prior late filings: An automatic waiver and abatement of penalties for tax year 2019 and 2020 returns that were filed by September 30, 2022 applies under IRS Notice 2022-36. This relief applies to Forms 1040, 1120, 1120-S, and 1065. It does not apply to Forms 990, 1041 or 706.

Lookback periods for refund claims extended: On February 27, 2023, the IRS issued Notice 2023-21, providing relief with respect to lookback periods for claims for credit or refund for returns with due dates postponed due to COVID-19. Due to the COVID-19 pandemic, the IRS postponed federal tax return filing and payment obligations that were due to be performed on or after April 1, 2020, and before July 15, 2020, to July 15, 2020. The IRS also postponed due dates and payment dates for Form 1040 with an original due date of April 15, 2021 to May 17, 2021. As a result of this Notice, the applicable refund period statute of limitations period for these tax years will start with the revised (later) COVID-19 dates and not from the original (pre-COVID extended) due dates.

Form 1099-MISC, Form 1099-NEC: These forms and instructions have been converted from an annual revision to continuous use. Both the forms and instructions will be updated as needed.

Form 1099-K: The reporting requirement for Form 1099-K, Payment Card and Third-Party Network Transactions, was reduced for tax year 2022 by the *American Rescue Plan of 2021*. However, on December 23, 2022, the IRS announced a delay in the new 1099-K reporting threshold for third-party settlement organizations (TPSOs). This means that for tax year 2022, the previous Form 1099-K reporting threshold of $20,000 in payments and/or over 200 transactions will remain in effect.

E-file Application Changes: On September 25, 2022, the IRS implemented a new electronic fingerprinting process for EFIN applications. Each new Principal and Responsible Official listed on a new e-file application, or added to an existing application, is required to schedule an appointment with Fieldprint®, the IRS authorized vendor (if the applicant is not an EA, CPA, or attorney). Prior to this date, the IRS had been relying on fingerprint cards for conducting background checks on tax practitioners. The IRS will not process fingerprint cards postmarked after August 15, 2022.

Internet platform for Form 1099 filings: The Taxpayer First Act required the IRS to develop an Internet portal by January 1, 2023. The new Information Returns Intake System (IRIS) went live on January 25, 2023, and will be available to replace the current system: Filing Information Returns Electronically (FIRE). Currently, IRIS will accept Forms 1099 only for tax year 2022 and later. The FIRE system also remains open for the filing of Forms 1099 and other information returns through at least the end of current filing season.[1]

---

[1] Taxpayer Advocate Service's 2022 Annual Report to Congress (ARC), Publication 2104. Also see Publication 5717, IRIS Taxpayer Portal User Guide.

Efile Procedure: Approximately 92 percent of individual taxpayers e-filed during processing year (PY) 2022.[2]

"Perfection Periods" for Rejected Submissions: The IRS provides a "transmission perfection period" for rejected returns. Individual returns are given a 5-day perfection period, while most business returns are given a 10-day perfection period; however, the Transmission Perfection Period for an extension to file Form 4868, 7004, or 8868 is five days.

ID Verification: On February 21, 2022, the IRS announced that it put new features in place for IRS Online Account registration. The IRS has two options for customers to sign up for IRS online accounts without the use of any biometric data, including facial recognition.

- **Without using biometric data** – Taxpayers will have the option of verifying their identity during a live, virtual interview with agents, using no biometric data.

- **Using biometric data** – Taxpayers will still have the option to verify their identity automatically through the use of biometric verification. For taxpayers who select this option, new requirements are in place to ensure images provided are deleted for the account being created.

Prior biometric data stored, including files that were already collected from customers who previously created an IRS Online Account, will be permanently deleted by March 11, 2022.

Due Diligence Preparer Penalty (6695(g)): The penalty for failure to meet the due diligence requirements on tax returns containing EITC, CTC/ACTC/ODC, the AOTC, and/or HOH status filed for 2022 is $560 per failure.

Form 1040-X and Direct Deposit: The Internal Revenue Service announced on February 9, 2023 that taxpayers electronically filing their Form 1040-X, Amended U.S Individual Income Tax Return, will for the first time be able to select direct deposit for their refund.

Form 1024 for Nonprofit Exemptions: Electronic filing of Form 1024, *Application for Recognition of Exemption Under Section 501(a) or Section 521 of the Internal Revenue Code*, was made mandatory upon the release of Revenue Procedure 2022-08 on January 3, 2022.[3] The form and user fee must be submitted online on www.pay.gov. The required user fee for Form 1024 is $600 for 2022.

---

[2] Taxpayer Advocate Service's 2022 Annual Report to Congress (ARC), Publication 2104.
[3] Organizations applying for §501(c)(3) exempt status on Form 1023 have been required to file Form 1023 electronically since 2020 per Revenue Procedure 2020-8.

New S Corporation Simplified Relief Procedure: On October 11, 2022, the IRS released Rev. Proc. 2022-19, which allows S corporations (or QSub parent) and their shareholders to obtain relief for certain matters without requesting a private letter ruling (PLR).

Tax Pro Accounts: The IRS recently launched Tax Pro Accounts, which lets tax professionals submit an authorization request to a taxpayer's IRS Online Account. This includes both power of attorney (Form 2848) and tax information authorization requests (Form 8821). Most requests record immediately to the CAF database. Taxpayers can then review, approve and sign the request electronically. IRS Publication 5533-A explains how to submit authorizations using a Tax Pro Account.

Extension of the Two-Year Carryover Period for EA Exam Candidates: The IRS has extended the two-year period to three years. For example, if a candidate passed Part 1 on November 15, 2020, then subsequently passed Part 2 on February 15, 2021, that candidate has until November 15, 2023, to pass the remaining part. Otherwise, the candidate loses credit for Part 1. The candidate has until February 15, 2024 to pass all other parts of the examination or will lose credit for Part 2.

Stalled E-file Mandates for Businesses: The *Taxpayer First Act of 2019*, authorized the IRS to issue regulations that would reduce the aggregate number of information returns that would trigger a mandatory efile requirement for most businesses. The Taxpayer First Act (TFA) included a phased threshold to require employers filing a certain number of information returns to do so electronically. On Feb. 23, 2023, The Department of the Treasury and the Internal Revenue Service published final regulations amending the rules for filing returns and other documents electronically. These regulations will require certain filers to e-file beginning in 2024. The final regulations:

- Reduce the 250-return threshold to generally require electronic filing by filers of 10 or more returns in a calendar year. The final regulations also create several new regulations to require e-filing of certain returns and other documents not previously required to be e-filed;

- Require filers to aggregate almost all information return types covered by the regulation to determine whether a filer meets the 10-return threshold and is required to e-file their information returns. Earlier regulations applied the 250-return threshold separately to each type of information return covered by the regulations;

- Eliminate the e-filing exception for income tax returns of corporations that report total assets under $10 million at the end of their taxable year, and

- Require partnerships with more than 100 partners to e-file information returns, and they require partnerships required to file at least 10 returns of any type during the calendar year to also e-file their partnership return.

Representation Practice Exams

Test Tip: Time yourself. Set up a watch or digital timer while you read and answer the questions. You will have 3.5 hours to take Part 3 of the EA exam—*Representation, Practices and Procedures*—with approximately two minutes to answer each question. Do not spend an inordinate amount of time on any one question and make sure to answer each one, even if you're not sure of the right answer. You can always mark the question for review and return later if you have time. All questions left blank are counted as wrong on the EA exam.

This page intentionally left blank.

#1 Sample Exam: Representation

(Please test yourself first, then check the correct answers at the end of this exam.)

1. Ariana is preparing her client's 2022 tax return. During the appointment, her client, Sergio, complains about the very small amount of compensation he received for serving on jury duty for all of May. Ariana does not ask about the jury duty pay, or report any income from jury duty on Sergio's tax return. Who can be subject to a penalty for willful understatement?

A. Sergio cannot be subject to a penalty for willful understatement, but Ariana can.
B. Ariana cannot be subject to a penalty for willful understatement, but Sergio can.
C. Ariana and Sergio both can be subject to a penalty for willful understatement.
D. Neither will be subject to a penalty for willful understatement, because jury duty is not taxable.

2. The IRS can certify a taxpayer has "seriously delinquent tax debt," which can lead to the denial and/or revocation of a taxpayer's passport, if the taxpayer owes more than how much in federal tax debt?

A. $10,000
B. $25,000
C. $26,000
D. $55,000

3. Which of the following statements regarding Circular 230 is <u>false?</u>

A. A criminal conviction for embezzlement is considered disreputable conduct under Circular 230.
B. Circular 230 never permits a practitioner to sign a return as a preparer if the return contains a frivolous position.
C. A practitioner is subject to sanction under Circular 230 if he or she does not receive proper consent to represent conflicting interests before the IRS.
D. The Circular 230 requirement that a practitioner exercise due diligence in preparing, approving, and filing returns does not apply if the practitioner is merely assisting in preparing or filing returns.

4. Some refund claims include extra due diligence requirements for tax preparers. Which of the following credits or tax situations do not have additional due diligence requirements?

A. Premium Tax Credit.
B. American Opportunity Tax Credit.
C. Additional Child Tax Credit.
D. Head of Household filing status.

5. A Circular 230 practitioner must, when requested by the Office of Professional Responsibility, provide OPR with any information he or she may have regarding a violation of Circular 230 regulations by any person, <u>except</u> in which of the following circumstances?

A. If the practitioner believes in good faith that such information is privileged.
B. If the practitioner has withdrawn from representation.
C. If the practitioner believes the request is of doubtful legality.
D. Both A and C are correct.

6. An electronically filed return is not considered "filed" until:

A. The electronic portion of the return has been submitted to the transmitter.
B. The electronic portion of the return has been rejected by the IRS.
C. The electronic portion of the return has been submitted to the IRS.
D. The electronic portion of the return has been acknowledged by the IRS.

7. All of the following are types of relief from "joint and several liability" except:

A. Separation of liability relief.
B. Equitable relief.
C. Equivalent relief.
D. Innocent spouse relief.

8. Married Filing Jointly means that the spouses _____.

A. Report their own incomes and deductions on separate returns.
B. Combine their income and deductions on the same return.
C. Combine their income, but not their deductions, on the same return.
D. Report their respective income as a qualified joint venture.

9. Roxanne is an enrolled agent. She has a new client, Michael, who informs her that he has a foreign bank account. Roxanne looks at the bank statements and determines that Michael has an FBAR reporting requirement. What is Roxanne required to do in this case?

A. Roxanne should prepare the FBAR return, or fire the client.
B. Roxanne must advise the client of his filing obligations. She is not obligated to prepare the FBAR for the client unless she feels competent to do so and the client has agreed to this additional service.
C. Roxanne should advise the client accordingly, and if the client refuses to allow her to file the FBAR, she should disengage.
D. Roxanne is required to file the FBAR, whether or not the taxpayer pays a fee for the service.

10. Andrew's total tax for 2022 is $1,600. He had $400 in withholding on his Form W-2. Andrew owes $1,200 when he files his return. His prior year's tax was $2,000. Will Andrew be subject to an estimated tax penalty?

A. Yes. He will owe a penalty.
B. No. He will not owe a penalty.
C. There is not enough information to make a determination.
D. He will not be charged a penalty as long as he pays all the tax owed when he files his return.

11. In order to determine if an individual taxpayer has a filing requirement, what information is required?

A. The taxpayer's income, filing status, and age.
B. The taxpayer's income, filing status, and place of birth.
C. The taxpayer's filing status and age.
D. The taxpayer's income and age.

12. Delia is a tax preparer who submits approximately 400 tax returns each year. Many tax returns that she prepares include claims for the Child Tax Credit and the Earned Income Credit, but she fails to submit Form 8867 to the IRS or do any due diligence for any of those returns. What potential preparer penalty does she face from the IRS?

A. $55 per failure.
B. $260 per return.
C. $560 per failure.
D. $5,000 per return.

13. Which IRS office administers the Annual Filing Season Program for tax return preparers?

A. The IRS Office of Appeals
B. The Office of Professional Responsibility
C. The Taxpayer Advocate's Office
D. The Return Preparer Office

14. A tax professional is required to determine a taxpayer's correct filing status. A taxpayer's filing status generally depends on whether the taxpayer is single or married. Whether a taxpayer is single or married is typically determined by _____.

A. The taxpayer's marital status at the beginning of the tax year.
B. The taxpayer's marital status at the end of the tax year.
C. The taxpayer's marital status in the middle of the year.
D. The taxpayer's marital status as determined by the courts.

15. Marika is trying to find tax law information about a specific tax issue for a deduction that she wants to take on her return. She's not sure if the deduction is valid. In order to avoid imposition of the accuracy-related penalty for a substantial understatement of income tax, which of the following is a type of authority may Marika rely on, in order to try to show substantial authority for her position on her tax return?

A. Revenue rulings.
B. IRS Form instructions.
C. Official IRS Publications.
D. Information on the IRS website.

16. Which of the following is an offense that could lead to practitioner sanctions by the OPR, according to Circular 230?

A. "Gross negligence"
B. "Gross recklessness"
C. "Gross incompetence"
D. "Gross delinquency"

17. Hunter took a large charitable deduction in a prior year, which was disallowed by the IRS when his return was audited. Hunter is assessed a penalty for substantial understatement of his income tax. An understatement is considered "substantial" if it is more than the larger of 10% of the correct tax or _____.

A. $1,000
B. $5,000
C. $10,000
D. $25,000

18. The Office of Professional Responsibility has initiated a disciplinary proceeding against Travis, who is an enrolled agent. Travis contends that he has done nothing wrong. What is OPR's burden of proof in a disciplinary proceeding against a tax practitioner?

A. OPR must prove by "clear and convincing evidence" that Travis willfully violated one or more provisions of Circular 230.
B. OPR must prove that Travis unintentionally violated one or more provisions of Circular 230.
C. OPR must prove by "clear and convincing evidence" that Travis willfully promoted a tax shelter.
D. OPR must prove that Travis negligently made inaccurate or unreasonable omissions on tax returns.

19. The Office of Professional Responsibility specifies many instances in which a practitioner might be sanctioned for incompetence or disreputable conduct. All of the following are listed except:

A. Promoting abusive tax shelters.
B. Threatening an IRS officer.
C. Aiding and abetting understatement of a tax liability.
D. Hiring an employee who has been censured by the IRS.

20. Enrolled agents who do not comply with the requirements for renewal of enrollment will be contacted by the Return Preparer Office. How much time does the EA have to respond to the RPO?

A. 30 days from the date of the notice.
B. 60 days from the date of the notice.
C. 60 days from the date of receipt.
D. 90 days from the date of the notice.

21. With regards to the IRS e-file program, what is a "Responsible Official?"

A. A Responsible Official is an individual with the authority to prepare refund advance loans.
B. A Responsible Official is an individual with the authority to sign tax returns.
C. A Responsible Official is an individual with primary authority over the Provider's IRS e-file operation at a location.
D. A Responsible Official is an individual with primary authority to collect taxpayer information and transmit completed tax returns.

22. Maximus argued his case before the U.S. Tax Court but took a patently frivolous position. What is the maximum penalty Maximus could face?

A. $1,000
B. $5,000
C. $10,000
D. $25,000

23. When a taxpayer submits an offer in compromise based on "doubt as to liability," which of the following is not required?

A. Application fee.
B. A written statement explaining why the tax debt or a portion of the debt is incorrect.
C. Form 656-L.
D. Taxpayer attestation and signature.

24. An enrolled agent is a person who has earned the privilege of representing taxpayers before the IRS by either: (1) passing a three-part examination, or (2) _____.

A. Through experience as a former IRS employee.
B. By going to an IRS-approved college.
C. By earning an accounting degree.
D. Through experience as a licensed auditor.

25. The IRS is auditing Wendy's chiropractic business. Wendy's business is an LLC that files a Schedule C. Of the following items, which in itself would not be adequate documentation to support her expenses on Schedule C?

A. A calendar that shows the time, place, date, and purpose of business meetings.
B. Copies of invoices and sales receipts provided to customers.
C. Mileage logs that show where, when, why, and how far she drove for business purposes.
D. Canceled checks.

26. A business entity may apply for an Employer Identification Number (EIN) online if their principal business activity is located in:

A. The United States or in any foreign country.
B. The United States, excluding U.S. Territories.
C. The United States or in any U.S. Territory or U.S. possession.
D. The continental U.S. only.

27. Which of the following designations is no longer recognized by the IRS?

A. Enrolled Agent
B. Enrolled Retirement Plan Agent
C. Enrolled Actuary
D. Registered Tax Return Preparer

28. Ayame is a nonresident alien who is a citizen of Japan. She does not have to pay U.S. federal income tax, but she does own a small number of U.S. investments. In 2022, she had a small amount of federal taxes withheld on income from a U.S. source investment. What can she do to receive a refund of her withheld taxes?

A. She must write a formal protest.
B. She must request a refund of incorrectly withheld amounts from the brokerage firm that holds the investment.
C. She must report the appropriate income and withholding amounts on Form 1040-NR.
D. She must file a refund claim on Form 1040.

29. Sabrina is an enrolled agent. She is in the process of representing Alexandra before the Internal Revenue Service for a tax matter. Alexandra's ex-husband, Paxton, also asked Sabrina to represent him for the same matter. Which of the following is not required for Sabrina to represent both?

A. Sabrina must notify the Office of Professional Responsibility that she will be representing both taxpayers.
B. Both taxpayers must waive the conflict of interest and give informed consent in writing to Sabrina.
C. Sabrina must reasonably believe that she will be able to provide competent and diligent representation to both taxpayers.
D. The representation is not prohibited by law.

30. Which disciplinary action(s) by the IRS is not recorded in the Internal Revenue Bulletin?

A. Reprimand.
B. Reprimand and censure.
C. Reprimand, censure, and suspension.
D. Only disbarments are recorded in the Internal Revenue Bulletin.

31. Which of the following is illegal under the Internal Revenue Code?

A. Tax avoidance.
B. Tax evasion.
C. Possessing offshore bank accounts.
D. Possessing foreign trusts.

32. Hamad is employed by a tax preparation firm. He is directly supervised by an EA in the firm who signs the tax returns that Hamad has prepared. Hamad:

A. Needs to obtain a PTIN.
B. Is only required to obtain a PTIN if he prepares a "substantial portion" of a client's tax return.
C. Is not required to obtain a PTIN because he does not sign the tax returns himself.
D. Is not required to obtain a PTIN because he is not yet a practitioner.

33. A fiduciary of a trust is treated by the IRS as _____.

A. The grantor of the trust.
B. A limited partner.
C. The taxpayer themselves.
D. The beneficiary of the trust.

34. Willow prepares her current year tax return and is owed a refund of $1,200. However, she owes delinquent federal taxes of $390 from an earlier tax year. Willow requests direct deposit of her refund. What will happen to her refund?

A. Her refund will be held until the overdue balance from the prior year is paid in full.
B. After her past due amount is offset, the balance will be deposited into her bank account.
C. After her past due amount is offset, the balance will be sent as a paper check, since the refund amount cannot be legally altered when a taxpayer chooses direct deposit.
D. Her refund will be held indefinitely pending official IRS review.

35. The more commonly used name of a Statutory Notice of Deficiency is:

A. CP-2000.
B. 30-day letter.
C. 90-day letter.
D. A federal tax levy.

36. Kendra is an enrolled agent. Kendra prepares a tax return for Richard, her new client. Kendra learns that Richard does not have a bank account to receive a direct deposit of his refund. Richard is distraught when Kendra tells him a paper refund check will take three or four weeks longer than the refund being direct deposited. Richard asks Kendra if she can deposit his tax refund into her bank account and then turn the money over to him when she gets it. What should Kendra do?

A. Kendra can offer to use her account to receive the direct deposit, and turn the money over to Richard once the refund is deposited.
B. Kendra can explain that a taxpayer's federal or state refund cannot be deposited into a tax preparer's bank account and he will have to open an account in his own name to have the refund direct deposited.
C. Kendra can suggest he borrow a bank account number from a friend because the taxpayer's name does not need to be on the bank account.
D. Kendra can suggest he borrow a bank account number from a family member because the taxpayer's name does not need to be on the bank account if the bank account belongs to a related person.

37. Which governmental organization administers and enforces the regulations governing practice before the IRS?

A. The Office of Professional Responsibility.
B. The Return Preparer Office.
C. Treasury Inspector General for Tax Administration.
D. The Taxpayer Advocate's Office.

38. Which of the following is considered a primary authority of U.S. tax law?

A. Supreme Court cases.
B. A professional law review.
C. International court cases.
D. U.S. Tax Court cases.

39. Russell is a taxpayer who filed an appeal of an IRS examination. He signed IRS Form 8821, *Tax Information Authorization*, for his tax preparer, Emily. Which of the following is correct?

A. Emily may represent Russell before IRS Appeals based on the Form 8821.
B. Emily may represent Russell before IRS Appeals with the oral consent of the client.
C. Emily may represent Russell before IRS Appeals with a note attached by the client.
D. Emily may not represent the client before IRS Appeals.

40. Julian's business records and computer were completely destroyed by a house fire. He loses all his records, so he tries to recreate his records using estimates, but he has no substantiation or receipts. Lilly is an enrolled agent that prepares Julian's return using estimates. What should Lilly do in this case?

A. Lilly cannot prepare a tax return using only estimates.
B. Lilly may prepare the tax return using reasonable estimates.
C. Julian must request a Private Letter Ruling if he is using estimates.
D. Lilly should refer Julian to a tax attorney.

41. Ahmed, an enrolled agent, prepared an individual income tax return for Camille. Camille has a balance due of $25,597. Camille is not able to pay the entire amount upon filing and would like to set up an installment agreement. Which of the following statements are correct with regards to this agreement?

A. Since Camille owes more than $25,000, she may not apply for an installment agreement.
B. Camille will not be charged a user fee to set up this installment agreement.
C. Camille must be in filing compliance.
D. Camille will not be charged interest and penalties while making installment payments.

42. An enrolled agent (EA) can represent a taxpayer:

A. Before IRS collections, examinations, and U.S. Tax Court.
B. Only if the EA prepared the return.
C. At all tax-related federal court proceedings.
D. Before any administrative level of the IRS.

43. An enrolled agent is normally not eligible to practice before:

A. An IRS revenue agent.
B. An IRS revenue officer.
C. A U.S. Tax Court judge.
D. An IRS appeals officer.

44. Rohan is an enrolled agent who takes a continuing education class on federal taxes. The class consists of two 90-minute segments at a conference. How many CE hours will be credited to Rohan for the course?

A. One.
B. Two.
C. Three.
D. Four.

45. Jayden filed his tax return on a timely basis. His refund was offset. He is not sure what type of debt was responsible for the offset, but he does owe delinquent student loans. What is the most likely scenario?

A. Jayden's IRS refund was offset to pay his overdue student loans.
B. Jayden's refund was transferred to Direct Pay.
C. Jayden's refund was sent to the wrong bank.
D. Jayden's refund was retained for future liability.

46. Which of the following types of tax advice is specific advice provided by the IRS to a taxpayer for a fee?

A. Revenue rulings.
B. Technical advice memoranda.
C. Private letter rulings.
D. Chief Counsel advice.

47. The IRS uses Collection Financial Standards to help determine a taxpayer's ability to pay a delinquent tax liability. National Standards have been established for five necessary expenses. Which of the following is not considered a "necessary expense" for IRS purposes?

A. Food.
B. Housekeeping supplies.
C. Personal care products.
D. Entertainment.

48. After an assessment, the Internal Revenue Service generally has the authority to collect outstanding federal taxes for how many years?

A. Five years.
B. Ten years.
C. Fifteen years.
D. Twenty years.

49. Hoshi is an enrolled agent, and she employs several tax preparers in her firm. One of Hoshi's employees prepares a return for a client. The return is later selected for examination, and one of the larger deductions is disallowed. Hoshi will not be subject to a preparer penalty if:

A. She does not sign the return and instead directs her employee to sign it.
B. There was a reasonable basis for the position.
C. She warned the preparer that the deduction was an aggressive position to take.
D. The preparer based the return on the information provided by the client.

50. In preparing an Earned Income Credit Worksheet and Form 8867, how long should a tax preparer retain copies of both documents?

A. One year from the filing of the return.
B. Two years from the filing of the return.
C. Three years from the filing of the return.
D. Six years from the filing of the return.

51. A new client, Samir, visits Deana, an enrolled agent. Samir believes that the U.S. tax system is purely voluntary and filed a return showing no income tax, requesting all withholding be refunded. The IRS assessed a $5,000 frivolous return penalty. Samir has received a Notice of Intent to Levy and Right to Collection Due Process (CDP) Hearing concerning the $5,000 penalty. Samir wants Deana to present his previous arguments about the tax system. Which of the following is a correct statement regarding the CDP hearing request raising arguments previously deemed frivolous?

A. If the appeal is deemed frivolous, Samir will be given 30 days to withdraw or amend the CDP appeal.
B. The EA would not be subject to a frivolous return penalty by submitting the CDP hearing request.
C. Since a $5,000 return penalty has been assessed, a second penalty cannot be assessed for the same tax period.
D. In all circumstances, filing the CDP request will suspend any levies while Appeals considers the request.

52. Tiffany is provided a $300 per month mileage allowance for business travel from her employer. In order for this monthly allowance to be non-taxable to Tiffany, which of the following is true?

A. Tiffany must return any excess reimbursement within 180 days after the expense was paid or incurred.
B. Tiffany must adequately account for the expenses within 60 days after they were paid or incurred.
C. Tiffany must receive the advance within 60 days of the time the taxpayer has the expense.
D. Tiffany must adequately account for the expenses within 30 days after they were paid or incurred.

53. Isabelle is an enrolled agent. Her client, Frederick, is requesting her assistance with a proposed accuracy-related penalty in an examination. All of the following are methods of addressing the penalty, EXCEPT:

A. Prior to a penalty being assessed, it may be appealed via deficiency procedures.
B. After the penalty has been assessed, a written request for abatement can be submitted.
C. After the penalty has been assessed and paid, Isabelle can prepare a claim for refund.
D. Prior to assessment, Isabelle can request binding arbitration to reconsider the penalty.

54. Alaina, an enrolled agent, represented her client, Inigo, and his former business partner, Danny, before the Internal Revenue Service with regard to a partnership tax matter. Due to the potential conflict of interest, Alaina obtained written consent from each of her clients, waiving the conflict of interest and giving informed consent. Alaina must keep those written consents for how long after the conclusion of representation?

A. 24 Months.
B. 36 Months.
C. 48 Months.
D. 72 Months.

55. Everett is an unenrolled return preparer. He has a PTIN, but he does not have an AFSP certificate. Which of the following statements is correct?

A. Everett may prepare and sign a taxpayer's return. However, he may not represent taxpayers before the Internal Revenue Service.
B. Everett may prepare tax returns, but he is only permitted to appear as a taxpayers' representative before a Customer Service Representative of the Internal Revenue Service.
C. Everett may receive refund checks on behalf of the taxpayer if Form 8821 has been executed.
D. Everett is permitted to represent a taxpayer over the telephone with the Automated Collection System unit, as long as he is listed as a third-party designee on the return.

56. Casimir, an enrolled agent, is representing a married couple, Nathan and Henrietta, in an ongoing IRS examination. One afternoon, Henrietta shows up early to a meeting at the EA's office. Off the record, Henrietta confides to Casimir that the examination is causing marital strife, and that Henrietta is not sure but now suspects that Nathan may have taken erroneous business deductions on his Schedule C. All of the following activities would address the conflict of interest EXCEPT (choose the best answer):

A. Politely advising Henrietta that this meeting was not appropriate, and make sure that no further meetings occur unless both spouses are present.
B. Informing both spouses of the potential ability to seek an innocent spouse determination as part of this examination as it moves forward.
C. Advising both spouses that there could be a conflict of interest going forward in representing both of them, and they may wish to retain their own counsel in the matter.
D. If Henrietta does not consent to Casimir sharing her concerns with her husband, Casimir cannot obtain informed consent from the husband to continue to represent both spouses without violating her confidences. Casimir should withdraw from representation of either spouse in order to avoid a lawsuit.

57. The U.S. Tax Court has generally held that taxpayers who rely on software to justify errors on self-prepared returns are:

A. Not liable for the Sec. 6662 accuracy-related penalty.
B. Liable for the Sec. 6662 accuracy-related penalty.
C. Liable for 20% of the Sec. 6662 accuracy-related penalty.
D. Liable for 40% of the Sec. 6662 accuracy-related penalty.

58. Only taxpayers who file electronically can pay an amount due by:

A. Check.
B. Money order.
C. Credit card.
D. Electronic funds withdrawal, with the submission of the return itself.

59. Francine plans to amend a prior-year return due to a loss on worthless securities. How long does she have to amend her tax return with regards to worthless securities?

A. 3 years
B. 5 years
C. 7 years
D. 10 years

60. Damian received a statutory Notice of Deficiency in 2022. Damian ignores the notice and does not contact the IRS or timely file a petition with the Tax Court. What will happen next?

A. The Internal Revenue Service will issue a 30-day letter.
B. The Internal Revenue Service will assess the tax it says Damian owes.
C. The Internal Revenue Service will issue a levy notice.
D. Damian will be required to post a deposit before being allowed to request an extension for time to file a petition.

61. When a taxpayer is required to file an FBAR and does not file the report, the person is potentially subject to:

A. Civil penalties only for non-filing.
B. Civil and criminal penalties for non-filing.
C. Criminal penalties only for non-filing.
D. Censure for non-filing.

62. Geena is expecting a tax refund of $5,400 this year. She chooses to direct deposit her refund. With regard to direct deposit, which of the following options is <u>not</u> permitted?

A. She may split the refund between two savings accounts.
B. She can purchase U.S. savings bonds with her refund.
C. She can have her refund directly deposited to a foreign bank account.
D. She can have her refund deposited onto a prepaid debit card.

63. The "declaration of representative" accompanying a power of attorney must be signed under penalties of perjury with the practitioner declaring that:

A. The taxpayer and the preparer are both aware of Circular 230 regulations.
B. The practitioner has never been under suspension or disbarment from practice before the Internal Revenue Service.
C. The practitioner is authorized to represent the taxpayer identified in the power of attorney for the matters specified therein.
D. The taxpayer did not sign the power of attorney under duress.

64. In which of the following scenarios could a taxpayer qualify for the Child Tax Credit?

A. Parent has an SSN, Child has an SSN.
B. Parent has an SSN, Child has an ITIN.
C. Parent has an ITIN, Child has an ITIN.
D. All of the above.

65. Marion is an enrolled agent. She has a client named Leonardo, who has several unpaid invoices. Marion prepared Leonardo's tax return and called him to pick it up. Later that week, Leonardo comes to Marion's office and demands the return of his records. He refuses to pay for any outstanding invoices. What is Marion required to do in this case?

A. Marion must promptly return any and all records belonging to the client that are necessary for him to comply with his federal tax obligations. She is not required to give Leonardo the tax return that she prepared.
B. Marion must promptly return any and all records, including the tax return that she prepared, regardless of any fee dispute.
C. Marion is not required to return the client's records while there is an ongoing fee dispute.
D. Marion is required to return the client's records only when the client pays in full.

66. What is EFTPS?

A. EFTPS is a banking application for IRS payments.
B. A secure IRS system for contacting taxpayers via email.
C. The official name of the IRS's e-file system.
D. EFTPS is a federal tax payment system that allows individuals and businesses to pay taxes online.

67. In determining whether or not a person qualifies for Head of Household filing status, which of the following is NOT one of the tests?

A. Marital status.
B. Qualifying person.
C. Cost of keeping up a home.
D. Income.

68. Which of the following would be an acceptable basis for an IRS appeal?

A. An appeal based on political grounds.
B. An appeal based on a recent court case.
C. An appeal based on religious grounds.
D. An appeal based on moral grounds.

69. Which of the following constitutes a violation by a tax preparer of Circular 230?

A. Advertising to existing clients.
B. Charging a contingent fee in connection with a refund claim filed for penalties or interest.
C. Filing a tax return with a mathematical error.
D. Giving written tax advice based on audit probability.

70. Lazaro is an enrolled agent who was referred to the Office of Professional Responsibility for preparer misconduct. What type of sanction will not be imposed against Lazaro by the OPR?

A. Disbarment.
B. Suspension.
C. Incarceration.
D. Censure.

71. Braxton files his tax return and is owed a $3,000 refund. He would like to purchase U.S. savings bonds with his refund. What kind of U.S. savings bonds can Braxton buy automatically using his tax refund?

A. Municipal bonds.
B. Series I U.S. savings bonds.
C. War bonds.
D. Series EE U.S. savings bonds.

72. When does a durable power of attorney expire?

A. When a taxpayer either marries or divorces.
B. When a taxpayer is deemed incompetent.
C. When a taxpayer becomes mentally incapacitated.
D. When a taxpayer dies.

73. A tax preparer is required to sign the preparer's section on each tax return that they prepare for compensation. The preparer's declaration on signing the return states that the information contained in the return is true, correct, and complete based on all information he has. This preparer statement is signed _____.

A. Under duress.
B. Without prejudice.
C. Without requirements.
D. Under penalties of perjury.

74. Which of the following infractions could cause an e-file provider to be permanently expelled from the IRS e-file program?

A. Level One.
B. Level Two.
C. Level Three.
D. All of the above.

75. Amos received a notice from the IRS saying a prior year's tax return had been examined, creating a tax assessment of $2,560. Amos disagrees with the amount of tax assessed. Amos could request audit reconsideration in all of the following situations EXCEPT when:

A. The full amount owed has already been paid.
B. There is new documentation for the examination.
C. Amos neither appeared for the examination nor sent information to the IRS.
D. Amos moved and never received the examination notice.

76. Brenda had her wallet stolen in January 2022, and now she is worried about identity theft and refund fraud. What should Brenda consider doing to minimize the risk of refund fraud?

A. Brenda should file a police report and file her tax return on paper.
B. Brenda should file an extension and wait to file her return until the extended due date.
C. Brenda should request an IP PIN and file her tax return as late as possible in the tax season.
D. Brenda should request an IP PIN and file her tax return as early as possible in the tax season.

77. How often must enrolled agents renew their enrollment?

A. Every year
B. Every two years
C. Every three years
D. Every five years

78. In which of the following instances does the IRS not require additional documentary evidence to support a taxpayer's travel, gift, or transportation expenses when he is traveling away from home on business?

A. A business meal expense of $250.
B. An expense of $150 for lodging while traveling on business.
C. Per diem allowances for meals or lodging that are reported to an employer under an accountable plan.
D. Auto expenses for travel from multiple work locations.

79. Which IRS insignia may an enrolled agent use in their advertising?

A. The official IRS e-file logo.
B. The U.S. Treasury seal.
C. The IRS eagle insignia.
D. The IRS Financial Management Service insignia.

80. The statute of limitations for the criminal offense of willfully attempting to evade or defeat any tax is:

A. Three years.
B. Six years.
C. Ten years.
D. Fifteen years.

81. Fidel is an enrolled agent. He comes into his office one morning and realizes that he has had a data breach—a scammer has logged into his computers remotely and submitted fraudulent returns under his EFIN. How long does Fidel have to contact the IRS to notify them of the breach?

A. One day.
B. Two days.
C. Three days.
D. Five days.

82. What is the function of an IP PIN?

A. The IP PIN acts as a fraud prevention tool to validate the dependents listed on the tax return.
B. The IP PIN acts as an authentication number to validate the correct owner of the Social Security number(s) listed on the tax return.
C. The IP PIN acts as an authentication number to validate the taxpayer's eligibility for refundable credits.
D. The IP PIN acts as a substitute for an electronic signature on an e-filed return.

83. What does Form 8879 authorize?

A. Transcript request.
B. E-file signature authorization by an ERO.
C. Extension of time to e-file.
D. Third Party Authorization.

84. Weston recently passed all three parts of the EA exam. He wants to submit his application to become an enrolled agent. With regards to his enrollment, what types of personal tax issues could negatively impact Weston's application for enrollment?

A. Lack of an Employer Identification Number.
B. Lack of a Social Security number.
C. An overdue tax return that has not been filed.
D. Weston does not have an EFIN.

85. A partnership with _____ or fewer partners is not required to e-file its tax return.

A. 50
B. 100
C. 200
D. 250

86. Carlisle is an enrolled agent. Carlisle has a new client named Monique who received an assessment from the IRS regarding a joint return she filed in a prior year with her ex-husband, Darby. During the interview, Carlisle learns that Darby was a gambling addict. Upon further examination of Monique's IRS transcripts, Carlisle discovers several more items of income that were left off the original return, and all of them were related to Darby's gambling habit. Monique had no idea that the return she filed had underreported income. Does Monique have any recourse in this case?

A. Monique and her ex-husband are both jointly and severally liable for the tax on the previously filed return, and she has no recourse in this case.
B. Monique may qualify for relief as an injured spouse.
C. Monique may qualify for relief as an innocent spouse.
D. Monique may request a conference with the IRS Appeals Office.

87. How does a taxpayer submit additional documentation to the IRS on an e-filed tax return?

A. The taxpayer should use Form 8453 and mail in supporting documentation.
B. A Form 1040-X must be filed with the paper attachments.
C. The taxpayer should use Form 2848 and mail in supporting documentation.
D. The return must be paper-filed if additional documentation must be sent with the return.

88. A case in the U.S. Tax Court is commenced by _____.

A. The filing of a petition.
B. A formal protest.
C. A taxpayer's appeal.
D. An IRS impasse.

89. Heartland Realty, LLP is a domestic partnership. Which of the following would prevent Heartland Realty from *electing out* of the "Centralized Partnership Audit Regime?"

A. Heartland Realty has 100 partners.
B. Heartland Realty has a partner that is a C corporation.
C. Heartland Realty has a partner that is a single-member LLC.
D. Heartland Realty has a partner that is an S corporation.

90. What is the legal procedure by which the IRS can seize a taxpayer's property in order to satisfy a tax debt?

A. A levy.
B. A jeopardy assessment.
C. A lien.
D. A deficiency seizure.

91. The IRS conducts a suitability check on all EFIN applicants. Suitability checks may include which of the following?

A. A drug check.
B. A residency check.
C. A criminal background check.
D. A DMV driving record check.

92. Faustino filed his federal tax return on time, and was expecting a $4,000 refund. However, his entire refund was offset to pay off his past-due debts. Which of the following would not be a reason for the IRS to offset Faustino's return?

A. Faustino has past-due federal taxes.
B. Faustino has unpaid local utility bills.
C. Faustino has delinquent student loans.
D. Faustino has past-due state income tax obligations.

93. Daniella is a tax professional who prepares over 300 tax returns every year. As such, she is subject to the e-file mandate. She has a new client, Fernando, who refuses to e-file his tax return. What is the proper action for Daniella to take in this case?

A. If her client refuses to e-file, Daniella must decline the engagement.
B. She must refer Fernando to a different tax return preparer.
C. She can prepare Fernando's return on paper and attach Form 8948.
D. She should encourage Fernando to file electronically. If he refuses, Daniella does not need to sign the return as a paid preparer.

94. The following tax professionals have unlimited representation rights before the IRS EXCEPT:

A. Enrolled agents.
B. Attorneys.
C. Certified Public Accountants.
D. AFSP certificate holders.

95. Which of the following is not exempt from IRS levy?

A. Wages.
B. Undelivered mail.
C. Unemployment benefits.
D. Child support.

96. What happens when the IRS files a "substitute return" for a taxpayer?

A. A substitute return will give the taxpayer credit for all exemptions, credits, and deductions he is entitled to receive. The taxpayer may not file his own tax return if a substitute return was filed.
B. A substitute return will give the taxpayer credit for all exemptions, credits, and deductions he is entitled to receive. The taxpayer may still file his own tax return, and the IRS will generally adjust the account to reflect the correct figures if the taxpayer has evidence of additional items to reduce the tax owed.
C. A substitute return may not give the taxpayer credit for all exemptions, credits, and deductions he is entitled to receive. The taxpayer may still file his own tax return to take advantage of any exemptions, credits, and deductions he is entitled to receive. The IRS will generally adjust the account to reflect the correct figures.
D. A substitute return may not give the taxpayer credit for all exemptions, credits, and deductions he is entitled to receive. The taxpayer may not file his own tax return if a substitute return has been filed.

97. Katie and Easton are married and file jointly. Easton is in the U.S. Marines, currently serving in a combat zone. Katie has not been able to contact her husband for several months. When one spouse is serving in a combat zone, what is required in order to file a joint return?

A. Both spouses must sign, so Katie must appeal to the IRS for a special exemption.
B. Katie may delay filing the tax return until Michael has returned to the United States and can sign the return.
C. Katie may sign the joint return on her husband's behalf, but only if she secured a power of attorney in advance.
D. Katie may sign on behalf of her husband, whether or not she has a signed power of attorney.

98. Estelle is an enrolled agent who obtained a signed Form 2848 from her client and would like to have it processed as soon as possible. How can she submit this form to the IRS for processing?

A. Estelle can email the form to the IRS.
B. Estelle can fax, mail, or upload the form on the IRS website.
C. Estelle can only submit the Form 2848 by mail.
D. In order to prevent fraud, Estelle cannot submit the form herself. Her client must submit the form to the IRS.

99. Marcel's tax return was chosen for audit. He tried to contact the revenue agent in charge of his case several times over a number of days, but the agent won't return any of his calls. Marcel then attempts multiple times to talk with the revenue agent's supervisor, leaving messages on her voicemail over a period of days, but also with no response. Marcel believes the IRS is not handling his case in a timely and appropriate manner. Who should be contacted for assistance?

A. IRS Help Line.
B. U.S. Tax Court.
C. Taxpayer Advocate Service.
D. IRS Appeals office.

100. Gustavo's tax return was audited and he vehemently disagrees with the auditor's findings. He gets a 90-day letter three months later. Gustavo wants to contest the assessment in court. Which of the following is a *benefit* for Gustavo to file a petition in the U.S. Tax Court for his proposed deficiency (as opposed to other available Federal court systems)?

A. Gustavo does not have to pay his contested tax first.
B. Gustavo can appeal his decision back to IRS Appeals if the judge rules against him.
C. Gustavo can contest tax deficiencies of any type or amount.
D. Gustavo can use an enrolled agent to represent him in court.

Please review your answer choices with the correct answers in the next section.

Answers to Exam #1: Representation

1. The answer is C. Ariana and Sergio both can be subject to a penalty for willful understatement. Since Sergio mentioned the jury duty during the tax interview, Ariana cannot ignore the implications of that information. The understatement on the return (omission of the jury duty pay) was due to Ariana's negligence or intentional disregard of rules or regulations.

2. The answer is D. A provision in the *Fixing America's Surface Transportation Act* (the FAST Act) gives power to the Internal Revenue Service to authorize the U.S. State Department to suspend or deny delinquent taxpayers' passport privileges. The U.S. State Department also will not issue a passport to anyone who currently owes more than the threshold amount. The IRS must first file a lien. The threshold in 2022 is $55,000, which includes penalties and interest. This amount is adjusted for inflation each year.

3. The answer is D. The Circular 230 requirement that a practitioner exercise due diligence in preparing, approving, and filing returns does apply, even if the practitioner is merely assisting in preparing or filing returns.

4. The answer is A. A tax preparer has additional due diligence requirements related to EITC, AOTC, and ACTC/CTC claims. The Tax Cuts and Jobs Act amended IRC §6695 to add due diligence requirements for the head of household (HOH) filing. Only the Premium Tax Credit does not have these "additional" due diligence requirements, although a tax preparer must always use reasonable care when preparing a tax return.

5. The answer is D. The answers "A" and "C" are correct; a Circular 230 practitioner must, when requested by the Office of Professional Responsibility, provide OPR with any information he or she may have regarding a violation of Circular 230 regulations by any person. An exception to this duty is made if (1) the practitioner believes in good faith and on reasonable grounds that such information is privileged or (2) that the request is of doubtful legality.

6. The answer is D. An electronically filed return is not considered "filed" until the electronic portion of the return has been acknowledged by the IRS. However, the date of the electronic postmark is considered the date of filing.

7. The answer is C. "Equivalent" relief does not exist. There are three types of relief from joint and several liability: (1) innocent spouse relief, (2) separation of liability relief, and (3) equitable relief. This is not the same as an "injured spouse" claim. An "injured spouse" claim is for allocation of a refund of a joint refund when the other spouse has a *separate* past-due federal tax, state tax, child or spousal support, or federal non-tax debt (such as a student loan).

8. The answer is B. "Married Filing Jointly" means that both spouses complete and sign the same tax return, combining their income and deductions on a single return. Both spouses are responsible for any tax owed on the return.

9. The answer is B. Roxanne must advise the client of his filing obligations. Roxanne is not obligated to prepare the FBAR unless she feels competent to do so and the client has agreed to this additional service. In the FBAR context, a practitioner acting as a preparer or advisor to a client may determine that one or more foreign accounts exist that must be reported in designated places on the client's tax return. If so, the practitioner should prepare the return or advise the client accordingly. Nevertheless, the practitioner does have an affirmative obligation to advise the client of the need to file an FBAR and the consequences of failing to file.

10. The answer is A. Andrew is liable for an estimated tax penalty because the amount he owes is over $1,000 and his withholding and credits are less than 90% of his current year tax or 100% of his prior-year tax.

11. The answer is A. To determine whether an individual taxpayer has a filing requirement, a preparer needs to know the taxpayer's income, filing status, and age.

12. The answer is C. In 2022, the IRS may assess a $560 penalty per failure against Delia, for not submitting the *Form 8867, Paid Preparer's Due Diligence Checklist*, with all EITC, AOTC, and CTC/ACTC claims. The Tax Cuts and Jobs Act also amended IRC section 6695 to add due diligence requirements for the head of household (HOH) filing.

13. The answer is D. The Return Preparer Office (RPO) oversees preparer tax identification numbers (PTINs), enrollment programs, IRS-approved continuing education providers, and the Annual Filing Season Program for tax return preparers.

14. The answer is B. A taxpayer's filing status generally depends on whether the taxpayer is single or married at the end of the year. The IRS has acknowledged that it recognizes the marital status of individuals as determined under state law in the administration of the Federal income tax laws (Rev. Rul. 2013-17).

15. The answer is A. Only the revenue rulings would be considered authority for meeting the "substantial authority" standard for a position taken on a tax return. "Substantial authority" does not include IRS forms or accompanying instructions, IRS publications, or information on the IRS website (this question is modified from a released EA exam question).

16. The answer is C. In determining sanctions, the IRS will consider a practitioner's pattern of conduct to assess whether it reflects "gross incompetence." Gross incompetence is defined as "gross indifference, preparation which is grossly inadequate under the circumstances, and a consistent failure to perform obligations to the client."

17. The answer is B. For individual taxpayers, an understatement is considered "substantial" if it is more than the *larger* of:

- 10% of the correct tax, or
- $5,000.

Under IRC §6662, the penalty for substantial understatement of income is calculated as a flat 20% of the net understatement of tax.

> **Note:** If a taxpayer's return claims a Section 199A deduction, then the 10% threshold above is reduced to 5%, for the determination of a penalty for substantial understatement.

18. The answer is A. For OPR to prevail in a disciplinary proceeding, OPR must prove by "clear and convincing evidence" that Travis willfully violated one or more provisions of Circular 230. Willful is defined as a voluntary, intentional violation of a known legal duty. Simple negligence is not the same as willful misconduct. Not all tax shelters are illegal, so simply promoting a tax shelter would not necessarily be classified as misconduct in a disciplinary proceeding.

19. The answer is D. Although hiring a suspended or disbarred practitioner is grounds for discipline, hiring an individual who has been *censured* by the IRS is not a sanctionable offense. Hiring an employee who is a former practitioner who has been *disbarred* or *suspended* is not permitted.

20. The answer is B. Enrolled agents who fail to comply with the requirements for eligibility for renewal of enrollment will be notified by the Return Preparer Office by first class mail. The notice will explain the reason for noncompliance. The enrolled agent then has 60 days from the date of the notice to respond.

21. The answer is C. A "Responsible Official" is an individual with the primary authority over the provider's IRS e-file operation at a location, is the first point of contact with the IRS, and has authority to sign revised IRS e-file applications (see Publication 3112, *IRS e-file Application and Participation*, for more information).

22. The answer is D. Under IRC section 6673, Maximus could face a penalty of up to $25,000 for making frivolous arguments before the United States Tax Court. Note that the IRS can assess a $5,000 penalty for frivolous tax returns, but the penalty for making a frivolous argument before the U.S. tax court is much higher.

23. The answer is A. In general, a taxpayer must submit an application fee with the submission of an Offer in Compromise. However, there are two exceptions to this requirement. First, no application fee is required if the OIC is based on *doubt as to liability.* Doubt as to liability exists where there is a genuine dispute as to the existence or amount of the correct tax debt under the law. Second, the fee isn't required if the taxpayer is an individual who qualifies as low-income. The low-income guidelines are included on Form 656.

24. The answer is A. An enrolled agent is a person who has earned the privilege of representing taxpayers before the Internal Revenue Service by either:

- Passing a three-part comprehensive IRS test, or
- Through experience as a former IRS employee (specifically, five years of continuous employment with the IRS during which time he must have been regularly engaged in applying and interpreting provisions of the Internal Revenue Code).

25. The answer is D. A canceled check, together with a bill from the payee, is ordinarily used to establish the cost of an item. However, a canceled check by itself does not prove a business expense without other evidence to show that it was for a business purpose. IRS Publication 535 states that a taxpayer must also substantiate the other elements of the expense, such as "time, place, and business purpose."

26. The answer is C. A taxpayer may apply for an EIN online if their principal business is located in the United States or in any U.S. Territory. Foreign business entities that have a U.S. filing obligation can obtain an Employer Identification Number (EIN) by completing Form SS-4.

27. The answer is D. Although still listed in the current version of Circular 230, the IRS no longer recognizes the Registered Tax Return Preparer (RTRP) designation. All the other designations listed in this question are recognized by the IRS.

> **Note:** Although the IRS no longer recognizes the RTRP designation, people who passed the RTRP exam in the past are allowed to participate in the IRS' AFSP program automatically. Unenrolled preparers who have passed the RTRP exam qualify for an exemption from the annual AFTR course but still must obtain 15 hours of continuing education.

28. The answer is C. Ayame must report the appropriate income and withholding amounts on Form 1040-NR. To claim a refund of federal taxes withheld on income from a U.S. source, a nonresident alien must report the appropriate income and withholding amounts on *Form 1040-NR, U.S. Nonresident Alien Income Tax Return.* The IRS will issue a refund, but it can take up to six months to process a Form 1040-NR return.

29. The answer is A. Sabrina is <u>not</u> required to notify the Office of Professional Responsibility that she will be representing both taxpayers. When there is a conflict of interest, the taxpayers involved must waive the conflict of interest and give informed consent in writing. The practitioner must reasonably believe that she will be able to provide competent and diligent representation to both taxpayers, and the representation cannot be prohibited by law. Sabrina must retain copies of the written consents for at least 36 months from the date of the conclusion of the representation or the date that the engagement ends. Requires written waivers/consents must be made available to the IRS upon request, but do not have to be submitted to the IRS or the Office of Professional responsibility.

30. The answer is A. A reprimand is the least severe sanction issued by the IRS. It is a private letter from the director of the OPR, stating the practitioner has committed some kind of misconduct under Circular 230. The practitioner's name is not published in the Internal Revenue Bulletin. Although the issuance of a reprimand is kept private, it stays on a practitioner's record. Censure, on the other hand, is a public reprimand, with the practitioner's name published in the Internal Revenue Bulletin.

31. The answer is B. Tax <u>evasion</u> is an illegal practice in which individuals or businesses intentionally avoid paying their true tax liabilities. Those caught evading taxes are subject to criminal charges and substantial penalties. Tax avoidance, though not specifically defined by the IRS, is commonly used to describe the legal reduction of taxable income, such as through deductions and credits. Taxpayers with offshore bank accounts and foreign trusts have additional reporting requirements, but the accounts themselves are not illegal, unless they are being used for tax evasion purposes.

32. The answer is A. Hamad is required to obtain a PTIN. Supervised preparers are still required to have PTINs. These are individuals who do not sign tax returns as paid return preparers but are:
- Employed by a law firm, EA office, or CPA practice, and
- Are directly supervised by an attorney, CPA, or EA who signs the returns prepared by the supervised preparer.

33. The answer is C. A fiduciary of an estate or trust is treated by the IRS as if he or she is **actually the taxpayer themselves.** A fiduciary automatically has both the right and the responsibility to undertake all actions the taxpayer is required to perform. For example, the fiduciary must file returns and pay any taxes due on behalf of the taxpayer (see *Instructions for Form 56* for more information).

34. The answer is B. After her past due amount is offset, the balance of her refund will be direct deposited into Willow's bank account. If a taxpayer's federal tax refund is decreased due to an offset, the refund will be decreased, and any remaining amount will be deposited into the taxpayer's designated account.

35. The answer is C. The Statutory Notice of Deficiency is often called the "90-day letter." It gives the taxpayer 90 days from the date of the notice to file a petition in the U.S. Tax Court challenging the proposed deficiency. A taxpayer has 150 days if his address is outside of the country on the day the notice of deficiency is mailed.

36. The answer is B. Kendra should explain that a taxpayer's federal or state refund cannot be deposited into a tax preparer's bank account. The client will have to open an account in his name to have the refund direct deposited.

37. The answer is A. The Office of Professional Responsibility (OPR) is in charge of administering and enforcing the regulations governing practice before the IRS.

38. The answer is A. Supreme Court cases are considered a primary authority of U.S. tax law. The IRS is always bound by law to follow U.S. Supreme Court decisions. However, the IRS is not required to follow the decisions of the other circuit courts or the Tax Court. Another primary tax authority is the actual Internal Revenue Code (IRC), which is enforced by the Internal Revenue Service (IRS) and decided by Congress. Examples of "secondary authority" include U.S. Tax Court cases and private letter rulings.

39. The answer is D. Emily cannot represent Russell because *Form 8821, Tax Information Authorization,* does not grant any type of representation rights. Emily would have to be an enrolled practitioner and obtain a signed Form 2848 from Russell in order to represent him before IRS appeals.

40. The answer is B. Lilly may prepare the return using reasonable estimates. She should disclose the use of estimates with a disclosure statement. IRC §274 generally prohibits claiming the following deductions unless substantiation requirements are maintained:
- Meals and entertainment
- Travel
- Gift Expenses
- Listed Property Expenses

However, estimates for these expenses are allowed if the taxpayer lost records due to fire, flood or another catastrophe. Since Julian lost his records during a house fire, he is permitted to use reasonable estimates, even for the expenses listed above.

> **Note:** The IRS states that, "the goal of record reconstruction is to use available documentation to develop a sound and reasonable estimate of the taxpayer's business income and expenses to support the tax return prepared. Although the taxpayer may not have formal books and records with supporting documentation, they may have partial records that can be used as a basis for reconstruction."[4]

41. The answer is C. Camille must be in filing compliance with all returns filed. If she is in filing compliance, she can apply for an installment agreement. In order for the IRS to grant a guaranteed installment agreement, a taxpayer must have not failed to file any income tax returns or pay any tax shown on such returns during any of the preceding five taxable years. There is a user fee to set up an installment agreement. (See Publication 594, *the IRS Collection Process*).

42. The answer is D. An enrolled agent can represent a taxpayer before any administrative level of the IRS.

---

[4] Based on the IRS EITC training document: "Schedule C and Record Reconstruction Training,"
See: https://www.eitc.irs.gov/eitc/files/downloads/Schedule_C_Training.pdf

43. The answer is C. An enrolled agent has unrestricted practice rights before all levels and all offices of the IRS. An enrolled agent is not eligible to practice before a U.S. district court judge or other judges in the U.S. court system. Only a licensed attorney has *automatic* practice rights before the U.S. courts, including the U.S. Tax Court. The only way an enrolled agent can represent a client in a U.S. Tax Court case is if he or she passes a U.S. Tax Court exam.

44. The answer is C. Rohan will earn three CE credits for the course. Continuing education credits are measured in "contact hours." A contact hour is defined as 50 minutes of continuous participation in a program. Credit is granted only for a full contact hour. Individual segments at a continuous conference will be considered one total program. For example, two 90-minute segments (180 minutes) at a continuous conference will count as three contact hours.

45. The answer is A. Jayden's IRS refund was likely offset to pay his overdue student loans. The U.S. Department of the Treasury's Bureau of the Fiscal Service (BFS) is authorized to collect delinquent tax debts as well as debts on behalf of other federal agencies. Through the offset program, BFS may reduce a taxpayer's refund and offset it to pay:

- Past-due child support;
- Federal agency non-tax debts;
- State income tax obligations; or
- Certain unemployment compensation debts owed to a state. Generally, these are debts for (1) compensation paid due to fraud, or (2) contributions owing to a state fund that were not paid).

46. The answer is C. Private letter rulings are written memoranda by the IRS in response to specific advice requests by taxpayers. Many private letter rulings cost well in excess of $10,000. Technical advice memoranda (TAM) are written memoranda furnished by the IRS upon request of a district director or a chief appeals officer pursuant to annual review procedures. Revenue rulings are official IRS pronouncements. Chief counsel advice (CCA) materials are written advice or instructions prepared by the Office of Chief Counsel and issued to employees of IRS field or service center offices or the Office of Chief Counsel.

47. The answer is D. Entertainment would not be a necessary expense. Collection Financial Standards are used to help determine a taxpayer's ability to pay a delinquent tax liability. Allowable living expenses include those expenses that meet the "necessary expense" test. The necessary expense test is defined as expenses that are necessary to provide for a taxpayer's (and family's) health and welfare and/or production of income. National Standards for food, clothing, and other items apply nationwide. National Standards have been established for five necessary expenses: food, housekeeping supplies, apparel and services, personal care products and services, and miscellaneous expenses. Out-of-pocket health care standards have also been established for out-of-pocket health care expenses, including medical services, prescription drugs, and medical supplies (e.g., eyeglasses, contact lenses, etc.).

48. The answer is B. Once an assessment is made, the IRS collection statute is typically ten years from the date of assessment. This is called the "collection statute expiration date" or "CSED." In certain situations, the CSED can be extended.

49. The answer is B. Hoshi will not be subject to a preparer penalty if any of the following apply:
- There was substantial authority for the position taken on the return.
- There was a reasonable basis for the position, and the position was adequately disclosed.
- There was reasonable cause for the underpayment and the preparer acted in good faith.

The determination of whether there was reasonable cause and/or a preparer acted in good faith is made on a case-by-case basis, taking into account all pertinent facts and circumstances. To meet the "reasonable basis" standard, a tax preparer may rely in good faith, without verification, on information furnished by a taxpayer, advisor, another preparer, or other party.

50. The answer is C. A tax preparer must retain the Earned Income Credit Worksheet and Form 8867 for any refundable claims of the EITC, CTC, ACTC, or AOTC a minimum of three years from the date of filing the return.

51. The answer is A. If the taxpayer requests a CDP hearing and provides frivolous arguments, in whole or in part, those arguments will not be heard. If the appeal is deemed frivolous, Samir will be given 30 days to withdraw or amend the CDP appeal.

52. The answer is B. In order for this monthly allowance to be non-taxable to Tiffany, she must adequately account for the expenses within 60 days after they were paid or incurred. This is an example of an accountable plan.

53. The answer is D. Isabelle **cannot** request binding arbitration to reconsider the penalty. The IRS takes penalty abatement requests on a case-by-case basis. Prior to a penalty being assessed in an examination, it may be appealed via deficiency procedures. After the penalty has been assessed, a written request for abatement can be submitted, or the EA can prepare a claim for refund if the penalty has been assessed and paid.

54. The answer is B. If there is a potential conflict of interest between two clients, Alaina must disclose the conflict and be given the opportunity to disclose all material facts. The written consent must be retained by Alaina for at least 36 months from the date representation ends. This question is based on an actual EA exam question.

55. The answer is A. Everett may prepare and sign a taxpayer's return. However, he may not represent taxpayers before the Internal Revenue Service. Note that even if Everett did have his AFSP certificate, he could only represent clients on examinations of returns that he prepared, as compared to EAs, CPAs, and attorneys, who can fully represent any taxpayer in all matters before the IRS (based on a released EA exam question).

56. The answer is A. The applicable reference is Circular 230, section 10.29. Circular 230 has several provisions related to conflicts of interest. A basic prohibition of the section is that: "a practitioner shall not represent a client before the Internal Revenue Service if the representation involves a conflict of interest." An exception to this rule applies ONLY when all of the following conditions are satisfied:

- The Practitioner must reasonably believe that he or she will be able to provide "competent and diligent representation" to each client represented;
- Representation of any of the clients is not prohibited by law; and
- Each affected client "waives the conflict of interest and gives informed consent, confirmed **in writing**" by the client(s). (This question is based on an actual EA exam question).

57. The answer is B. The Tax Court has generally held that taxpayers who rely on software to justify errors on self-prepared returns are liable for the Sec. 6662 accuracy-related penalty.[5]

58. The answer is D. Only taxpayers who file electronically can pay an amount due by electronic funds withdrawal (this is also called "direct debit") with the submission of the return itself.

59. The answer is C. Francine has seven years to amend in order to claim a loss for worthless securities. In general, a taxpayer should claim a loss on worthless stock in the year in which it becomes worthless. However, a taxpayer is allowed to amend a prior-year return up to *seven* years in the past. This is an exception to the normal statute of limitations for amended returns. The taxpayer must use *Form 1040-X, Amended U.S. Individual Income Tax Return*, to amend their return for the year the security became worthless. When the taxpayer amends a return to take a loss on worthless securities, the taxpayer must file within seven years from the date of the original return, or two years from the date the taxpayer paid the tax, whichever is later.

60. The answer is B. A notice of deficiency, also called a "statutory notice of deficiency" or "90-day letter," is a legal notice in which the IRS determines the taxpayer's tax deficiency. Damian ignored the notice, so the next thing that will occur is that the Internal Revenue Service will assess the tax it says Damian owes.

61. The answer is B. When a taxpayer is required to file an FBAR and does not file the report, the person is potentially subject to civil **and** criminal penalties for non-filing. The penalties for non-filing of an FBAR are extremely severe. Civil penalties apply to both willful and non-willful violations.

62. The answer is C. Geena cannot have her refund directly deposited into a foreign bank account. Refunds can be deposited into a U.S. financial account or prepaid debit card. Taxpayers can also choose to split their refund into separate bank accounts (but no more than three).

_____

[5] Anyika v. Commissioner, T.C. Memo. 2011-69

63. The answer is C. The "declaration of representative" accompanying a power of attorney must be signed under penalties of perjury with the practitioner declaring that the practitioner (or other representative) is <u>authorized</u> to represent the taxpayer identified in the power of attorney for the matters specified therein.

Part II	Declaration of Representative

Under penalties of perjury, by my signature below I declare that:

- I am not currently suspended or disbarred from practice, or ineligible for practice, before the Internal Revenue Service;
- I am subject to regulations in Circular 230 (31 CFR, Subtitle A, Part 10), as amended, governing practice before the Internal Revenue Service;
- I am authorized to represent the taxpayer identified in Part I for the matter(s) specified there; and
- I am one of the following:

  a Attorney—a member in good standing of the bar of the highest court of the jurisdiction shown below.

  b Certified Public Accountant—a holder of an active license to practice as a certified public accountant in the jurisdiction shown below.

  c Enrolled Agent—enrolled as an agent by the IRS per the requirements of Circular 230.

  d Officer—a bona fide officer of the taxpayer organization.

  e Full-Time Employee—a full-time employee of the taxpayer.

  f Family Member—a member of the taxpayer's immediate family (spouse, parent, child, grandparent, grandchild, step-parent, step-child, brother, or sister).

  g Enrolled Actuary—enrolled as an actuary by the Joint Board for the Enrollment of Actuaries under 29 U.S.C. 1242 (the authority to practice before the IRS is limited by section 10.3(d) of Circular 230).

  h Unenrolled Return Preparer—Authority to practice before the IRS is limited. An unenrolled return preparer may represent, provided the preparer (1) prepared and signed the return or claim for refund (or prepared if there is no signature space on the form); (2) was eligible to sign the return or claim for refund; (3) has a valid PTIN; and (4) possesses the required Annual Filing Season Program Record of Completion(s). **See Special Rules and Requirements for Unenrolled Return Preparers** *in the instructions for additional information.*

  k Qualifying Student or Law Graduate—receives permission to represent taxpayers before the IRS by virtue of his/her status as a law, business, or accounting student, or law graduate working in a LITC or STCP. See instructions for Part II for additional information and requirements.

  r Enrolled Retirement Plan Agent—enrolled as a retirement plan agent under the requirements of Circular 230 (the authority to practice before the Internal Revenue Service is limited by section 10.3(e)).

  ▶ **IF THIS DECLARATION OF REPRESENTATIVE IS NOT COMPLETED, SIGNED, AND DATED, THE IRS WILL RETURN THE POWER OF ATTORNEY. REPRESENTATIVES MUST SIGN IN THE ORDER LISTED IN PART I, LINE 2.**

Note: For designations d–f, enter your title, position, or relationship to the taxpayer in the "Licensing jurisdiction" column.

Designation—Insert above letter **(a–r)**.	Licensing jurisdiction (State) or other licensing authority (if applicable)	Bar, license, certification, registration, or enrollment number (if applicable)	Signature	Date
C	IRS	00090111-EA	*Jane Smith, EA*	3/1/2023

64. The answer is A. The child must have a valid SSN to qualify for the Child Tax Credit. The SSN must be issued before the due date for the filing of the return for the taxable year. However, children who would otherwise qualify for the CTC, except that they lack an SSN, are eligible for the non-refundable $500 "Other Dependent Credit" (or ODC).

65. The answer is A. Marion must, at the request of her client, promptly return any and all original records that the client needs to comply with his federal tax obligations. This requirement does not include any forms or schedules the practitioner prepared because Marion is withholding these documents pending the client's payment. A practitioner is permitted to retain copies of the records returned to a client.

66. The answer is D. EFTPS (Electronic Federal Tax Payment System), is an online federal tax payment system that allows taxpayers to pay individual and business taxes online. Individuals can pay their quarterly estimated taxes, and they can make payments weekly, monthly, or quarterly. Businesses can schedule payments up to 120 days in advance of their tax due date. Individuals can schedule payments up to 365 days in advance of their tax due date.

67. The answer is D. A taxpayer's income level is irrelevant in the determination of Head of Household filing status. The client must pass the following three tests:

- Marital status (be unmarried or "considered unmarried").
- Have a qualifying person that lives in the home.
- Must pay over one-half of the cost of keeping up a home where a qualifying person resides.

68. The answer is B. Reasons for an appeal must be supported by tax law, including recent court cases or any other relevant tax law changes. An appeal cannot be based solely on moral, religious, political, constitutional, conscientious, or similar grounds. IRS Appeals is a venue where disagreements concerning the application of tax law can be resolved on an impartial basis without having to go to court.

69. The answer is D. When giving written tax advice, a tax practitioner must not take into account the possibility that a tax return will not be audited or that a matter will not be raised on audit in evaluating a Federal tax matter (i.e., audit lottery). Answer "A" is incorrect, because advertising to clients is not a violation. Answer "B" is incorrect because a contingent fee can be charged, among other situations, in connection with a refund claim filed for penalties or interest. Answer "C" is incorrect, because filing a return with a mathematical error is not a violation if the error was not willful.

70. The answer is C. OPR sanctions include disbarment, suspension, and censure. Although a tax preparer may be subject to criminal prosecution and even incarceration in some cases, the Office of Professional Responsibility would not be responsible for applying any criminal penalties.

71. The answer is B. Braxton can automatically purchase Series I U.S. Savings Bonds using his tax refund, if he wishes. Taxpayers can buy savings bonds in increments of $50. Series I Savings Bonds, also known as I bonds, can only be bought directly from the U.S. Treasury Department. Up to $5,000 of I bonds can be purchased from a Federal tax refund.

72. The answer is D. A durable power of attorney is terminated upon a taxpayer's death. A durable power of attorney is not subject to a time limit and will continue in force after the incapacitation or incompetency of the individual. An IRS power of attorney is automatically revoked if the person who made it is found to be incompetent, but a durable power of attorney can only be revoked by the person who made it, and while that person is mentally competent.

73. The answer is D. This preparer statement on the return is signed under penalty of perjury. The taxpayer also signs the jurat on the taxpayer's signature area of the return, and the preparer's area of the jurat is signed under penalty of perjury, as well.

74. The answer is C. The IRS can sanction any e-file provider who fails to comply with e-file regulations. The IRS categorizes the seriousness of infractions as Level One (the least serious), Level Two, and Level Three (the most serious). A Level One infraction may result in an e-file provider receiving a written reprimand from the IRS. A Level Two infraction may result in a provider being suspended from participation in e-file for one year. A Level Three infraction may result in a provider being suspended from participating in e-file for two years or permanently expelled from the program. Level three infractions include:

- Association with known criminals.
- Monetary crimes.
- Fiduciary crimes.
- Conduct indicative of potential fraudulent acts, (e.g., directing all or a portion of the taxpayer's refund via direct deposit to the preparer's bank account or negotiating the taxpayer's refund check).
- Any criminal conduct.

75. The answer is A. Amos could request an audit reconsideration except when the full amount owed has already been paid (see IRS Publication 3598, *The Audit Reconsideration Process*). This question is based on a released EA exam question.

76. The answer is D. Brenda should request an IP PIN and file her tax return as early as possible in the tax season. All taxpayers are now eligible for an IP PIN. Stolen Identity Refund Fraud (SIRF) is a growing type of crime that occurs when thieves file fraudulent refund claims using a legitimate taxpayer's identifying information, such as Social Security numbers that they have stolen. Typically, SIRF perpetrators file the false returns electronically, early in the tax filing season so that the IRS receives the false SIRF return before the legitimate holder of the Social Security number has time to file his return. A legitimate taxpayer who is owed a refund can help prevent SIRF by filing his tax return early.

77. The answer is C. Enrolled agents must renew their enrollment status every three years. As part of the application process, the IRS checks the candidate's filing history to verify that he has filed his federal returns and paid applicable taxes.

78. The answer is C. The responsibility to prove entries, deductions, and statements made on your tax returns is known as the "burden of proof." Taxpayers generally must have documentary evidence, such as receipts, canceled checks, or bills, to substantiate their expenses. However, documentary evidence is not needed if any of the following conditions apply:

- The taxpayer has meals or lodging expenses while traveling away from home for which he reports to his employer using a *per diem* allowance method under an accountable plan.
- The taxpayer's expense, other than lodging, is less than $75.
- The taxpayer has a transportation expense for which a receipt is not readily available. However, in the case of mileage, the taxpayer should keep a mileage log.

79. The answer is A. Practitioners generally may not use official IRS insignia in their advertising. However, a practitioner may use the IRS e-file logo. The IRS e-file logo cannot be combined with the IRS eagle symbol, the word "federal," or with other words or symbols that suggest a special relationship between the IRS and the practitioner. Advertising materials must not carry the FMS (IRS Financial Management Service), IRS, or other Treasury seals.

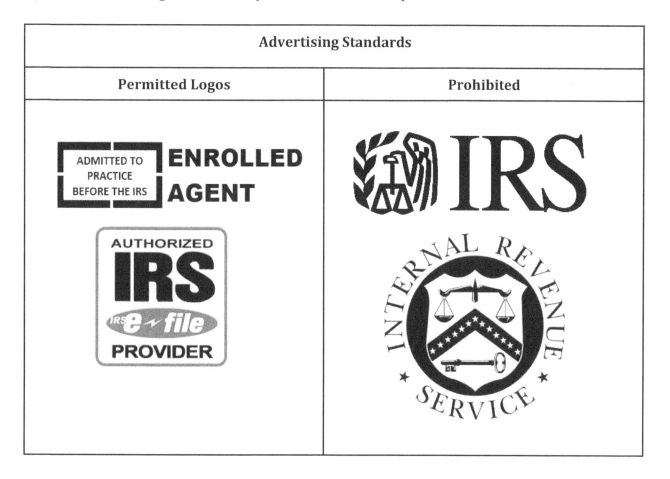

80. The answer is B. Under IRC section 6531 (periods of limitation on *criminal* prosecutions), there is a six-year statute of limitations for the criminal offense of willfully attempting to evade or defeat any tax. Do not confuse this with the *collection statute* on a fraudulent return. There is no statute of limitations for collection when a fraudulent return is filed, but the collection statute is a *civil* matter, not a criminal one.

81. The answer is A. Fidel has <u>one day</u> to contact the IRS to report the data breach. In case of a data breach, a tax preparer has one day to contact the IRS. *Publication 5199, Tax Preparer Guide to Identity Theft,* outlines the warning signs that indicate individual and business clients' Social Security numbers have been compromised, as well as the steps that must be taken in the case of a data breach. Also, see IRS *Publication 4557, Safeguarding Taxpayer Data,* for more information on data security for tax professionals.

82. The answer is B. The IP PIN acts as an authentication number to validate the correct owner of the Social Security number(s) listed on the tax return. The IRS IP PIN is a 6-digit number assigned to eligible taxpayers to help prevent the misuse of their Social Security number on fraudulent federal income tax returns. A new IP PIN will be generated each year.

83. The answer is B. A taxpayer may authorize an electronic return originator (ERO) to enter his PIN for him by signing *Form 8879, IRS e-file Signature Authorization.* Tax preparers must ensure that they receive signed authorizations from their clients before electronically submitting the clients' tax returns.

84. The answer is C. An overdue tax return could impact Weston's application for enrollment. In general, any overdue tax return that has not been filed could negatively impact a practitioner's application for enrollment. Lack of a Social Security number, EIN, or EFIN would not automatically preclude a tax professional from enrollment. For example, specified tax return preparers who live and work abroad are not precluded from enrollment, even if they do not have an SSN.

85. The answer is B. Partnerships with *more than* 100 partners are required to e-file their partnership tax return. Partnerships with 100 or fewer partners (Schedules K-1) may voluntarily file their returns electronically, but are not required to do so.

86. The answer is C. Monique may qualify for relief as an innocent spouse even when she is responsible for all or part of the tax liability. A spouse requesting innocent spouse relief must not have known, or have reason to have known, that the income of the *other* spouse was underreported or that the tax shown on the return was otherwise incorrect. The taxpayer must complete and attach *Form 8857, Request for Innocent Spouse Relief,* to apply for innocent spouse relief.

Note: An "injured" spouse claim is different from an "innocent spouse" relief request. Form 8379 allows an injured spouse to request the division of the tax overpayment attributed to each spouse. An innocent spouse uses *Form 8857, Request for Innocent Spouse Relief,* to request relief from joint liability for tax, interest, and penalties on a joint return for items of the other spouse (or former spouse) that were incorrectly reported on a joint return.

87. The answer is A. *Form 8453, U.S. Individual Income Tax Transmittal for an IRS e-file Return,* is used to send any required paper forms or supporting documentation that may be needed with an e-filed return. Form 8453 must be submitted to the IRS within three business days after receiving acknowledgment that the IRS has accepted the electronically filed return. An example of when this form might be required is when a taxpayer donates a used vehicle to a charity and receives *Form 1098-C, Contributions of Motor Vehicles, Boats, and Airplanes.* The taxpayer's return can be e-filed, claiming the deduction, and the Form 1098-C can be mailed in by itself, along with the Form 8453.

88. The answer is A. A case in the U.S. Tax Court is commenced by the filing of a Tax Court petition. The petition must be timely filed within the allowable time. There are no extensions for filing a petition. The Tax Court cannot extend the time for filing a petition, which is dictated by statute.

89. The answer is C. Heartland Realty cannot *elect out* of the Centralized Partnership Audit regime if it has a partner that is a single-member LLC. In order to "elect out" of the Centralized Partnership Audit regime, the partnership must have 100 *or fewer* partners (exactly 100 partners would be permissible), and the partners must be "permitted partners." Permitted partners include only: individuals, C corporations, S corporations, and estates of deceased partners (but not bankruptcy estates).

90. The answer is A. The Internal Revenue Service may use a levy to legally seize a taxpayer's property to satisfy a tax debt. A levy is a legal seizure of property. An IRS lien is the precursor to an IRS levy. The lien is a claim used for security of the tax debt.

91. The answer is C. The IRS conducts a suitability check on all EFIN applicants and on all Principals and Responsible Officials listed on the EFIN application. Suitability checks *may include* all the following:

- A criminal background check.
- A credit history check.
- A tax compliance check to ensure that all required returns are filed and paid, and to identify assessed fraud penalties.
- A check for prior non-compliance with IRS e-file requirements.

92. The answer is B. Faustino's unpaid utility bills would not be included in the IRS's refund offset program. All or part of a taxpayer's refund may be used (offset) to pay off past-due federal tax, unpaid state income tax, state unemployment compensation debts, child support, spousal support, or other federal non-tax debts, such as delinquent student loans.

93. The answer is C. Daniella may still prepare Fernando's return. She should attach Form 8948, *Preparer Explanation for Not Filing Electronically*, to her client's paper return. Any tax preparer who files 11 or more Forms 1040 or Forms 1041 (combined) during a calendar year must use IRS e-file. However, clients themselves may choose not to e-file their returns.

94. The answer is D. AFSP certificate holders only have *limited* representation rights. Enrolled agents, certified public accountants, and attorneys have unlimited representation rights before the IRS. Tax professionals with these credentials may represent their clients on any matter, including audits, payment issues, collection issues, and appeals.

95. The answer is A. Wages are subject to IRS levy. So are Social Security payments and other federal payments. Financial accounts, retirement accounts, and brokerage accounts can also be levied. The following items are <u>exempt</u> from an IRS levy:

- Wearing apparel and school books.
- Fuel, provisions (food), furniture, personal effects in the taxpayer's household, arms for personal use, or livestock.
- Books and tools necessary for the trade, business, or profession of the taxpayer.
- Undelivered mail.
- Unemployment benefits.
- Workers' compensation, including amounts payable to dependents.
- Certain annuity or pension payments, but only if payable by the Army, Navy, Air Force, Coast Guard, or under the Railroad Retirement Act or Railroad Unemployment Insurance Act. Traditional or Roth IRAs are not exempt from levy.
- Judgments for the support of minor children (child support).
- Certain public assistance and welfare payments and amounts payable for Supplemental Security Income for the aged, blind, and disabled under the Social Security Act.

96. The answer is C. If a taxpayer fails to file an income tax return, the IRS can file a substitute return (SFR) for him. The IRS will then send a notice of deficiency (90-day letter) proposing a tax assessment. A substitute return may not provide the taxpayer all the exemptions, credits, and deductions he is entitled to receive. However, if the IRS files a substitute return, a taxpayer can still file his own return to take advantage of exemptions, deductions, and credits. The IRS will generally adjust a taxpayer's account to reflect the correct figures.

97. The answer is D. Katie is allowed to sign on behalf of her husband whether or not she has a signed power of attorney. A spouse can sign a joint return for a spouse who cannot sign because he is serving in a combat zone, even without a power of attorney.

Note: This exception is *specifically* for personnel serving in a combat zone and does not apply to civilians or taxpayers who are simply active-duty military. For members of the Armed Forces serving in a combat zone or qualified hazardous duty area, the deadline for filing tax returns, paying taxes, filing claims for refunds, and taking other actions with the IRS is automatically extended. For more information, see *IRS Publication 3, Armed Forces' Tax Guide.*

98. The answer is B. Estelle can fax, mail, or upload the form on the IRS website. The "Submit Forms 2848 and 8821 Online" tool is available on the *www.IRS.gov/taxpros* page. Tax professionals must have an account, including a current username and password, in order to submit these forms online.

Note: The IRS recently launched Tax Pro Accounts, which lets tax professionals submit an authorization request to a taxpayer's IRS Online Account. This includes both power of attorney (Form 2848) and tax information authorization requests (Form 8821). Taxpayers can then review, approve and sign the request electronically.

99. The answer is C. In this situation, as Marcel has repeatedly contacted the appropriate people at the IRS without any response, Marcel should contact the Taxpayer Advocate Service. Congress created the Taxpayer Advocate Service, an independent function within the IRS, to help taxpayers resolve issues with the IRS. If a taxpayer has a problem that is not being resolved in a timely manner, (for example, an amended return that is taking much longer than normal to process, or a tax refund that has not been released, even months after the return was filed), then the taxpayer can contact the Taxpayer Advocate Service to intervene.

100. The answer is A. One advantage of the U.S. Tax Court over the U.S. Court of Federal Claims or U.S. District Court is that Gustavo is not required to pay the contested tax first (as he must when filing a case in these other U.S. courts).

#2 Sample Exam: Representation

(Please test yourself first, then check the correct answers at the end of this exam.)

1. Which of the below statements is correct regarding complaints for the sanctioning of a practitioner, employer, firm, appraiser, or other entity practicing before the Internal Revenue Service?

A. A United States Tax Court judge oversees proceedings regarding the complaint.
B. In general, discovery may be permitted at the discretion of an Administrative Law Judge.
C. Within 30 days of receipt of the answer, the presiding judge will notify the parties of the right to request discovery and the timeframe for filing a request.
D. The complaint can only be served on the respondent in person by a designated employee of the Internal Revenue Service.

2. Luther is an enrolled agent who was subject to a disbarment proceeding. The administrative law judge upheld the OPR's decision to disbar him from practice. Does Luther have any appeal rights at this point?

A. Within 60 days after the administrative law judge makes a decision on a disciplinary action, Luther may appeal the decision to the Return Preparer Office.
B. Within 60 days after the administrative law judge makes a decision on a disciplinary action, Luther may appeal the decision to the Treasury Appellate Authority.
C. Within 30 days after the administrative law judge makes a decision on a disciplinary action, Luther may appeal the decision to the Treasury Appellate Authority.
D. No, Luther does not have any appeal rights after the administrative law judge makes his decision.

3. In which of the following situations must a tax return preparer obtain client consent to disclose or receive sensitive tax return information?

A. The preparer receives a grand jury subpoena requesting client records.
B. A preparer reports a possible crime to authorities involving one of their clients.
C. For purposes of peer reviews.
D. None of the above disclosures requires permission from a client.

4. Agustina is an enrolled agent. Which of the following actions is she not permitted to do?

A. Prepare a formal written protest on behalf of a client to request an appeals conference.
B. Submit an e-filed return for a client who is domiciled overseas.
C. Negotiate a taxpayer's refund check, as long as she has the client's written permission.
D. Represent a taxpayer before IRS collections.

5. The IRS' e-file rules prohibit a tax preparer from:

A. Filing a return in early January using a client's last pay stub for wage information, if the taxpayer has not yet received his Form W-2.
B. Specifying that the IRS direct deposit a client's tax refund to the client's checking account.
C. Charging a separate fee to e-file.
D. All of the above.

6. A Statutory Notice of Deficiency is also known as a 90-day letter because:

A. The taxpayer has 90 days from the date of the letter to request a Collection Appeals hearing.
B. The taxpayer has 90 days from the date of the letter to file a formal protest with TIGTA.
C. The taxpayer has 90 days from the date of the letter to file a protest with the IRS Office of Appeals.
D. The taxpayer has 90 days from the date of the letter to file a petition with the United States Tax Court.

7. Joey received an examination notice in 2022. During the examination of Joey's Form 1040, the IRS examiner found numerous errors resulting in additional tax. One of the adjustments was a large amount of unreported income discovered in a concealed bank account. Some deductions were supported with altered documents. Joey also gave false statements throughout the examination. All of the acts of the taxpayer, when seen as a whole, most likely indicate:

A. Negligence.
B. Fraud.
C. Noncompliance.
D. A tax protester argument.

8. A single financial account is limited to _____ electronically deposited tax refunds per tax year.

A. One
B. Two
C. Three
D. No limit

9. Which of the following is not a reason for the IRS to abate interest on a taxpayer's tax liability?

A. Managerial act.
B. Ministerial act.
C. When the interest was incurred while the taxpayer was in a combat zone or federally declared disaster area.
D. Reasonable cause.

10. Which of the following documents can be used to verify a taxpayer's Social Security number and correct name spelling?

A. Driver's license.
B. Passport.
C. Social Security card.
D. Birth certificate.

11. Trent decided to represent himself in an IRS audit. When he arrived at the IRS office, he became agitated during the initial examination interview and requested to speak to a representative. Which of the following statements is correct?

A. The taxpayer may leave the examination and finish the audit through correspondence.
B. An IRS interview must be suspended when the taxpayer clearly requests the right to consult with a representative.
C. If the taxpayer chooses to suspend the interview, he must return in person with his representative.
D. The IRS is not required to cease an examination when the taxpayer requests a representative.

12. The IRS cannot issue refunds for 2022 tax returns before February 15, 2023, if those returns claim which of the following refundable credits?

A. The Retirement Savings Contributions Credit
B. The Credit for Excess Social Security and RRTA Tax Withheld
C. The Earned Income Tax Credit (EITC)
D. The Premium Tax Credit (PTC)

13. Which of the following taxpayer numbers is valid for claiming the Earned Income Tax Credit?

A. Social Security number.
B. Adoption taxpayer identification number.
C. Individual tax identification number.
D. Employer Identification Number.

14. Safeguarding of IRS e-file from fraud and abuse is the shared responsibility of:

A. The IRS and the Police.
B. The IRS and the FBI.
C. The IRS and Authorized IRS e-file Providers.
D. The Department of the U.S. Treasury and official tax software providers.

15. Patrick is a tax return preparer who accepts electronic signatures. He has a client who lives in a different state. How is Patrick required to authenticate the identity of the taxpayer?

A. The taxpayer must mail or fax a copy of his Social Security card to Patrick for review.
B. The taxpayer must mail or fax a copy of his driver's license, with a picture ID, to Patrick for review.
C. Patrick must verify that the name, Social Security number, address, date of birth, and other personal information provided by the taxpayer are consistent with information obtained through record checks with applicable agencies or institutions, or through credit bureaus or similar databases.
D. No special verification procedures are required.

16. Clarence is an enrolled agent. His new client, Chloe, wants to know if their discussions during normal tax preparation are privileged. What type of information or activities would *not* be privileged?

A. Communications pertaining to tax advice.
B. The preparation of Chloe's income tax return.
C. Non-criminal tax matters before the IRS.
D. Non-criminal tax proceedings in federal court actions.

17. ITINs automatically expire after _____ years of nonuse.

A. One
B. Two
C. Three
D. Five

18. In which of the following situations is an IRS power of attorney required?

A. Allowing the tax practitioner to receive, but not cash, taxpayer refund checks.
B. Allowing the IRS to discuss return information with a third-party designee.
C. Allowing a partnership representative to perform acts for the partnership.
D. Allowing the IRS to discuss return information with a fiduciary.

19. The IRS has the authority to issue a summons in all of the following instances except:

A. To prepare a substitute return when a taxpayer has not filed one.
B. To determine the liability of a taxpayer.
C. To collect any internal revenue tax liability.
D. To require a taxpayer to create a tax return when he has not filed one.

20. Which is the highest degree of tax authority for all taxpayers?

A. Treasury Department Regulations.
B. Revenue Rulings.
C. Private Letter Ruling.
D. The Internal Revenue Code.

21. A practitioner must submit records or information requested by the IRS unless the practitioner believes that the records are _____?

A. Confidential.
B. Protected.
C. Privileged.
D. Destroyed or missing.

22. What practice rights do all enrolled agents have?

A. Unlimited practice rights before the IRS.
B. Unlimited practice rights before the IRS and the U.S. Tax Court.
C. Limited practice rights before the IRS.
D. Unlimited practice rights before the U.S. Treasury Department.

23. The IRS may accept an offer in compromise based on three grounds. Which of the following is not a valid basis for submitting an offer in compromise to the IRS?

A. Doubt as to collectibility.
B. Effective tax administration.
C. Doubt as to liability.
D. Undue hardship.

24. In the previous year, Beverly filed an Innocent Spouse claim that was denied. She now has new additional information that may help her case; can she file a second claim?

A. No, Beverly cannot file a second Innocent Spouse Claim after an IRS denial.
B. Yes, Beverly can file a second claim, but the claim must be filed with the U.S. Tax Court.
C. Yes, Beverly can file a second claim. The second claim must be filed with the Taxpayer Advocate Office.
D. Yes, Beverly can file a second claim, provide the new additional information, and it will be reconsidered by the IRS. However, she normally cannot appeal the redetermination to the U.S. Tax Court.

25. Which type of practitioner fee is prohibited by Publication 1345, *Handbook for Authorized IRS e-file Providers?*

A. Charging a fee for direct deposit.
B. Fixed fees for bookkeeping services.
C. Hourly fee rates for tax consulting.
D. Charging a fee for e-filing a return.

26. Rosalee files jointly with her husband, who has delinquent student loans. Their entire tax refund is applied against his past-due student loans. Rosalee would like to claim her portion of their tax refund, so she files for _____ relief.

A. Innocent spouse.
B. Equitable relief.
C. Injured spouse.
D. Separation of liability.

27. Which of the following may the Internal Revenue Service settle by accepting an Offer in Compromise for less than the full amount of the balance due?

A. A tax deficiency, but never penalties or accrued interest.
B. A tax deficiency plus penalties, but not accrued interest.
C. A tax deficiency plus accrued interest, but not penalties.
D. A tax deficiency plus penalties and accrued interest.

28. Under Circular 230, in which of the following cases may the IRS suspend a certified public accountant from practice before the IRS?

A. The CPA moves outside the U.S. and attempts to represent overseas taxpayers.
B. The CPA's license is suspended by the board of accountancy for a matter unrelated to taxation.
C. The CPA takes an aggressive position on a tax return.
D. The CPA hires unenrolled preparers to work in his office.

29. As part of the application to become an authorized IRS e-services provider, which of the following categories of tax professionals is required to be fingerprinted?

A. Enrolled agents and unenrolled tax return preparers.
B. All e-services applicants must be fingerprinted by the IRS.
C. Unenrolled tax return preparers.
D. Only CPAs and tax attorneys must be fingerprinted because they are licensed by the state, not the federal government.

30. Betty is an enrolled agent who is cleaning up her office files and purging old records. When is the *earliest* she may shred the records related to her continuing education (CE)?

A. Four years following the date of the EA renewal for which the CE is credited.
B. Six years following the date of the EA renewal for which the CE is credited.
C. Immediately after the date of the EA renewal for which the CE is credited
D. Betty should not destroy her CE records as long as she is in active status.

31. In a prior year, Griffin's wife fraudulently sold his separate property but did not report the capital gain from the sale on their jointly-filed tax return. Griffin eventually files for divorce from his wife. Their joint return is later audited by the IRS, and the IRS determines that there was a substantial understatement of tax. What type of spousal relief may Griffin qualify for, in order to request relief from an understatement of tax on the jointly-filed return?

A. Economic hardship.
B. Separate liability relief.
C. Injured spouse relief.
D. Equitable relief.

32. A tax preparer must complete the paid preparer section of the tax return in which of the following scenarios?

A. An employee preparer who completes employment tax returns for his employer.
B. An enrolled agent who prepares her own tax return.
C. A CPA who prepares a return for her brother and charges him only a nominal fee.
D. An enrolled agent who prepares his father's return for free.

33. The statute of limitations on assessment increases to six years if there is an omission of more than _____ of the gross income stated on the return.

A. 15%
B. 25%
C. 50%
D. 75%

34. How long is an IRS power of attorney authorization valid?

A. Until the taxpayer's retirement.
B. For three years.
C. Until the close of the taxable year for which it was filed.
D. Until revoked or withdrawn.

35. A tax preparer who violates due diligence requirements for the EITC, AOTC, ACTC (or determination of Head of Household filing status) faces what penalty for tax year 2022?

A. $280 penalty for each failure.
B. $560 fine for each failure.
C. $750 fine for each failure.
D. $1,000 fine for each failure and imprisonment up to one year.

36. Sylvie, an enrolled agent, prepares William's income tax return. William gives Sylvie power of attorney, including the authorization to receive his federal income tax refund check. Accordingly, the IRS sends William's $1,000 refund check to Sylvie's office. William is very slow in paying his bills and owes Sylvie $500 for tax services. Sylvie should:

A. Use William's check as collateral for a loan to tide her over until William pays her.
B. Refuse to give William the check until he pays her the $500.
C. Turn the check directly over to William.
D. Get William's written authorization to endorse the check, cash the check, and reduce the amount William owes her.

37. Jeronimo's individual income tax return was under IRS examination. Five months before the expiration of the statute of limitations, the Revenue Agent wanted Jeronimo to agree to extend the statute of limitations. Which of the following is true?

A. Jeronimo does not have a right to refuse to extend the statute of limitations, if his return is still under examination.
B. The Revenue Agent must advise Jeronimo that he has a right to refuse to extend the statute of limitations, but if he does so, his case will be immediately referred to the U.S. Tax Court.
C. The Revenue Agent must advise Jeronimo that he has a right to either extend the statute of limitations, but if he does so, he must file a formal protest with the Secretary of the Treasury.
D. The Revenue Agent must advise Jeronimo that he has a right to refuse to extend the statute of limitations and if he does agree to an extension, the agreement can be restricted as to particular issues on the tax return.

38. Which of the following is an example of an individual filing a frivolous tax return?

A. A taxpayer who incorrectly claims the Earned Income Tax Credit when he is not eligible for it because he did not read the instructions carefully enough.
B. A taxpayer who files a tax return and strikes out the jurat.
C. A preparer who files a delinquent tax return because the taxpayer refused to file.
D. A fiduciary who files an incorrect tax return and later amends it.

39. In serving a complaint against a practitioner, the Office of Professional Responsibility may use all of the methods listed below except:

A. Private delivery service.
B. E-mail.
C. First class mail.
D. In person.

40. Rachel passed all three parts of the EA exam. When is she considered "officially enrolled"?

A. When the IRS issues her enrollment card.
B. When she submits Form 23, and the form is processed by the IRS.
C. When she goes through an IRS suitability check.
D. When she passes the final Special Enrollment Exam.

41. Which of the following fees would not be permitted under Circular 230?

A. A written schedule of hourly fees.
B. A flat fee for an initial consultation with a client.
C. Unconscionable fees for audit representation services.
D. A contingent fee based on an IRS examination of an original tax return.

42. Tasha's tax return was audited by the IRS. The IRS examiner found evidence of unreported income from illegal activities. The IRS issued an assessment, determining a substantial underpayment of tax on Tasha's tax return due to fraud. How much is the penalty added to her tax?

A. 20% of the underpayment, reduced for those items for which there was adequate disclosure
B. 50% of the underpayment due to fraud
C. 75% of the underpayment due to fraud
D. 100% added to any other penalty provided by law

43. Circular 230 states a practitioner may not willfully, recklessly, or through gross incompetence sign a tax return or claim for refund that the practitioner knows, or reasonably should have known, contains a position that:

A. Understates the liability for tax.
B. Is reckless or has intentional disregard of rules or regulations.
C. Lacks a reasonable basis.
D. All of the above.

44. Which of the following actions is not considered "disreputable conduct" by the IRS?

A. Willfully failing to e-file returns electronically if they fall under the e-filing mandate.
B. Failing to include a valid PTIN on tax returns.
C. Performance as a notary by a practitioner.
D. Willfully failing to file a tax return.

45. Dottie is a CPA. She is taking a position on a client's tax return that requires disclosure. Which form can be used to disclose a position on a tax return?

A. Form 8275
B. Form 8823
C. Form 656
D. Form 8821

46. A preparer is required to provide a copy of the tax return to a client. Which of the following is NOT required?

A. The preparer must provide a complete copy of the tax return to the taxpayer.
B. The tax return must be provided on paper.
C. The tax return must be provided along with a copy of the preparer's PTIN.
D. None of the above is correct.

47. Suzanne is an enrolled agent who is interviewing her new client, Jackson, who wants to claim the American Opportunity Tax Credit. Jackson has no proof that he was a student during the year, and other information Jackson offers seems incorrect to Suzanne. Under her due diligence requirements, what should she do?

A. Refuse to accept the engagement.
B. Report the client to the IRS fraud hotline.
C. Take note of the woman's inconsistent answers and go ahead and submit the claim anyway.
D. Ask additional questions if the information furnished seems incorrect or incomplete.

48. Amanda is an enrolled agent, and she prepares approximately 250 tax returns for compensation during the year. She is a U.S. citizen. Which of the following numbers is required in order for her to prepare tax returns for compensation?

A. An EFIN and a PTIN.
B. Only a PTIN.
C. A PTIN and an EIN.
D. An EFIN and an EIN.

49. What is a private letter ruling?

A. A private letter ruling becomes public once Tax Court litigation begins.
B. A private letter issued by the IRS Office of Appeals.
C. A response from Congress to the IRS to clarify Congressional action on a specific tax issue.
D. A communication from the Internal Revenue Service in response to a taxpayer's written request for guidance on a particular tax issue.

50. What is the dollar limit for a taxpayer to be eligible to request the U.S. Tax Court small case procedures?

A. $15,000
B. $25,000
C. $50,000
D. $100,000

51. Which of the following is *not* a type of Treasury regulation?

A. Legislative regulation
B. Congressional regulation
C. Interpretive regulation
D. Procedural regulation

52. Josiah is an enrolled agent. His new client, Paloma, asks Josiah to prepare her tax return. He requests her prior-year returns, and discovers that Paloma has failed to file tax returns for the prior three years. Paloma only wants Josiah to prepare the current year return. What is Josiah required to do in this scenario?

A. He must decline the engagement.
B. He must decline the engagement and report Paloma to the IRS for tax fraud.
C. He must advise Paloma that she did not comply with Federal tax law, and the consequences for not filing the returns.
D. He must report Paloma to the Office of Professional Responsibility.

53. Who is allowed to determine the time and place for an audit of a taxpayer?

A. The IRS.
B. The taxpayer.
C. The taxpayer's representative and the IRS have an equal say in the determination of the time and location of an audit.
D. The IRS, the taxpayer, and the taxpayer's representative have an equal say in determining the time and location of an audit.

54. A Third-Party Designee has the right to do which of the following tasks?

A. Sign a binding agreement for the taxpayer.
B. Respond to IRS notices about math errors, offsets, and return preparation.
C. Represent the taxpayer before the IRS.
D. Receive refund checks.

55. Alexander plans to e-file his federal tax return. He owns specified foreign assets and must file Form 8938, Statement of Specified Foreign Financial Assets, as well as the FBAR. What should he do to make sure his tax return filing is complete?

A. Attach Form 8938 and the FBAR to his federal return as a pdf attachment.
B. Attach only the FBAR to his federal return. The Form 8938 must be sent to the Financial Crimes Enforcement Network.
C. He must mail both forms separately to the Internal Revenue Service.
D. Attach only Form 8938 to his federal return and file the FBAR through the Financial Crimes Enforcement Network's E-Filing system.

56. Renata is an enrolled agent. Her client, Lucian, wants to use direct deposit. Which of the following statements about direct deposit is incorrect?

A. Lucian may designate refunds for direct deposit to a credit card account.
B. Renata must accept any direct deposit election to any financial institution designated by Lucian.
C. Lucian may designate refunds for direct deposit to up to three qualified accounts.
D. Lucian should not request a deposit of his refund to an account that is not in his name.

57. What is the purpose of a Centralized Authorization File (CAF) number?

A. It is an IRS file designed to prevent the theft of taxpayer identification numbers.
B. It is an IRS file containing the PTINs of all paid tax preparers.
C. It is an IRS file containing information from Forms 2848 only.
D. It is an IRS file containing authorization information from both Forms 2848 and Forms 8821.

58. The Annual Filing Season Program is a _____.

A. Mandatory program.
B. Voluntary program.
C. Volunteer program.
D. Charitable program.

59. Stacy is an enrolled agent with two clients who are both parties in the potential sale of a business. The sale is not prohibited by law. Stacy believes she can provide competent and diligent representation to each client. Which statement best describes the action Stacy must take to fulfill the requirements of Circular 230 before representing both clients?

A. Since she has already researched the situation and determined she is competent to handle the matter; Stacy is not required to take further action.
B. Stacy must obtain either oral or written permission from both clients, stating they have been made aware of the potential for conflict of interest.
C. Stacy must meet with both clients at the same time to inform them of the potential for conflict of interest.
D. Stacy must inform each client of the potential for conflict of interest and then obtain written waivers of the conflict from both clients.

60. Edward is a tax preparer. One of his client's returns was recently audited by the IRS, and a large penalty was assessed against the taxpayer. A few weeks later, Edward receives a letter from the IRS with a proposed §6694 penalty against him for understatement of a taxpayer's liability. Before Edward is formally assessed a penalty under IRC §6694, how many days does he have to file an appeal before the penalty is assessed?

A. 10 days
B. 30 days
C. 45 days
D. The penalty is assessed immediately and must be appealed retroactively

61. A "remote transaction" for electronic signature is one in which the taxpayer is electronically signing the signature authorization form and the ERO is not physically present with the taxpayer. For remote transactions, the ERO must record which of the following information?

A. The taxpayer's SSN and driver's license number.
B. The taxpayer's name, address, and a copy of his or her birth certificate.
C. The taxpayer's name, social security number, address and date of birth.
D. The taxpayer's name, social security number, address and driver's license number.

62. A taxpayer would like assistance from the Taxpayer Advocate Service. All of the following are considerations in determining whether a request will be granted EXCEPT:

A. The taxpayer will suffer irreparable harm or long-term adverse impact if relief is not granted.
B. The taxpayer is facing a significant and unexpected tax liability.
C. The taxpayer is experiencing economic harm or is about to suffer economic harm.
D. The taxpayer is facing an immediate threat of adverse action.

63. Natalie became an enrolled agent several years ago. For renewal purposes, what is the minimum number of hours of continuing education (CE) she must take each year?

A. She is required to take a minimum of 15 hours per year, two of which must be on ethics.
B. She is required to take a minimum of 16 hours per year, two of which must be on ethics.
C. She is required to take a minimum of 18 hours per year, four of which must be on ethics.
D. She is required to take a minimum of 24 hours per year, two of which must be on ethics.

64. A rejected electronic individual income tax return can be corrected and retransmitted without new signatures if changes do not differ from the amounts on the original electronic return by more than:

A. $50 of total income or AGI.
B. $100 of total income or AGI.
C. $500 of tax due or AGI.
D. A rejected e-file return cannot be retransmitted without new signatures.

65. Paul and Donatella are married but live separately. They choose to file jointly, but they want to split their refund between their respective checking accounts. How is this accomplished, if possible?

A. They must complete Form 8888, *Allocation of Refund (Including Savings Bond Purchases)*.
B. Splitting a refund is not possible.
C. This can only be accomplished if filing a paper return.
D. They must file separate tax returns if they wish to split their refund.

66. Which of the following is not an acceptable method for a taxpayer to sign a completed tax return?

A. Self-select PIN.
B. Practitioner PIN.
C. Identity Protection (IP) PIN.
D. Handwritten signature on a paper-filed return.

67. When the IRS rejects a return that an Electronic Return Originator (ERO) attempted to e-file for a taxpayer, the ERO must advise the taxpayer of the rejection and also provide the taxpayer with what additional information?

A. IRS Customer Service phone number for assistance.
B. Declaration Control Number.
C. IRS code section.
D. The reject code, accompanied by an explanation.

68. Which of the following sanctions will the Office of Professional Responsibility <u>not</u> impose on a practitioner?

A. Disbarment.
B. Censure.
C. Formal reprimand.
D. Criminal penalties.

69. All of the following are options for how a taxpayer may direct his tax refund except:

A. Receive the refund as a paper check.
B. Split the refund, with a portion applied to next year's estimated tax and the remainder received as direct deposit or a paper check.
C. Use the refund to purchase municipal bonds.
D. Use the refund (or part of it) to purchase U.S. Series I Savings Bonds.

70. For which of the following does the U.S. Tax Court NOT have jurisdiction?

A. Gift tax deficiencies.
B. Income tax deficiencies.
C. FBAR penalties.
D. Innocent spouse relief.

71. What penalty does a taxpayer who files a "frivolous" return potentially face?

A. $1,000
B. $5,000
C. $10,000
D. $100,000

72. Callum has a 25-year-old daughter named Genie. Callum has an accounting degree, but he is not an enrolled practitioner. Genie's tax return was chosen for examination by the IRS. Genie is not claimed as a dependent on Callum's tax return, and Callum is not an enrolled agent, attorney, or CPA. Which of the following statements is correct?

A. Callum may represent his daughter before the IRS if Genie signs a Form 2848.
B. Callum may not represent his daughter before the IRS because Genie is no longer a minor and Callum is not enrolled to practice before the IRS.
C. Callum may not represent his daughter because she is not his dependent.
D. Callum is not an enrolled preparer, so he may not represent an adult child because of privacy regulations and conflicts of interest.

73. Penny has an installment agreement in place with the IRS. On January 5, 2022, she gets into a bad car accident and misses a payment. The IRS sends her a notice 30 days later proposing to terminate her installment agreement. Which of the following statements is <u>correct?</u>

A. Penny has no appeal rights once the installment agreement is in default.
B. Penny may appeal the termination of her installment agreement.
C. Penny may appeal the termination, and the IRS will be prohibited from levying until 60 days after her appeal is completed.
D. Penny may appeal the termination by filing a petition with the U.S. Tax Court within 30 days of receipt of the notice.

74. Deborah is a tax preparer. She has a new client that does not have a Social Security card and is not eligible for a Social Security number. What type of documentation should she request from the taxpayer in this case?

A. A driver's license.
B. An ITIN card or letter.
C. A passport.
D. None of these documents are acceptable.

75. An IRS power of attorney must contain all of the following information except:

A. The type of tax involved.
B. The name and address of the representative.
C. The name and taxpayer identification number of the taxpayer.
D. The specific date the tax return was filed, if delinquent.

76. Which of the following can constitute a "reasonable basis" for a position taken on a tax return?

A. IRS publications.
B. IRS tax forms and instructions.
C. Congressional committee reports.
D. Internal Revenue Manual.

77. Under Circular 230, the definition of a "tax return" includes:

A. A claim for a refund, an original return, and an amended return.
B. An original return or an amended return.
C. A claim for a refund, an original return, and an extension request.
D. Only an original return.

78. Bianca is an enrolled agent, and Chandler is her client. Bianca submitted Chandler's tax return right on the filing deadline. The IRS rejected Chandler's return 24 hours later, and an extension was not filed for him. Bianca reviews the return with Chandler and finds that the e-file submission cannot be corrected and the return must go in on paper. When resubmitting the rejected return <u>as a paper return</u>, Chandler must file the return <u>no later</u> than:

A. The due date for filing the return.
B. The due date for filing the return or 5 calendar days after the return was rejected.
C. By the due date for filing the return or 10 calendar days after the return was rejected.
D. By the due date for filing the return or 15 calendar days after the return was rejected.

79. Which of the following individuals is **not** under the jurisdiction of Circular 230?

A. An enrolled agent who files Form 2848 for a client he is representing in an examination.
B. A licensed attorney that provides written tax advice, but does not prepare tax returns.
C. An enrolled agent who does representation work for clients before the IRS but does not prepare tax returns.
D. An employee of a tax preparation firm who collects receipts, organizes records, and gathers information for a practitioner.

80. Which of the following actions is always prohibited by Circular 230?

A. Charging contingent fees.
B. Notarizing documents for the clients that the practitioner represents before the IRS.
C. Representing two clients when there is a conflict of interest.
D. Promoting a tax shelter to an existing client.

81. Isidore is not an enrolled agent, CPA, or attorney, but she has a valid AFSP certificate. Lorenzo, the president of Carlsbad Engineering, Inc. hired Isidore to prepare the company's 2022 Form 1120-S. Isidore e-filed the corporate tax return for Carlsbad Engineering on February 15, 2023, signing it as the preparer. Lorenzo signed the return as the company's president. This is the only return Isidore prepared for Carlsbad Engineering. A year later, the IRS began an examination of Carlsbad Engineering's 2020, 2021, and 2022 Federal tax returns. Isidore has a power of attorney to represent Carlsbad Engineering, Inc. Under Circular 230, Isidore is permitted to represent Carlsbad Engineering during the examination with regard to its:

A. 2022 Form 1120-S only.
B. 2020, 2021, and 2022 Form 1120-S only.
C. 2020, 2021 Forms 1120-S.
D. None of the above.

82. Some unenrolled preparers are exempt from the Annual Filing Season course requirement because of their completion of other recognized state or national competency tests. Which of the following individuals would be required to complete the Annual Filing Season course in order to obtain an official Record of Completion?

A. A tax preparer who passed the Registered Tax Return Preparer exam.
B. Tax preparers who have passed the Special Enrollment Exam Part I within the past two years.
C. Volunteer Income Tax Assistance (VITA) volunteers.
D. Accounting students registered at a recognized educational institution.

83. Sterling is an enrolled agent. A long-time client starts a new business in an industry with numerous specialized tax regulations and incentives. Sterling begins working on the client's tax return but finds he does not understand most of the elections and credits that are applicable to the new business. Can Sterling prepare and sign this tax return with his current lack of understanding of tax rules that pertain to the client's business?

A. Yes. It is not unusual for a tax preparer to lack understanding in complex areas of tax law.
B. Yes, but only if Sterling has another tax practitioner from his firm review the return before Sterling signs it.
C. Yes, but only if Sterling accepts a reduced fee for the work from his client.
D. No. Sterling cannot prepare or sign a tax return if he lacks sufficient competence.

84. Calhoun owes $3,900 in federal income tax, but cannot pay the taxes due. He would like to apply for an installment agreement in order to pay over time. In which scenario could the IRS waive the user fees for Calhoun's installment agreement request?

A. Calhoun is a full-time student.
B. Calhoun's income is below 250% of the applicable federal poverty level.
C. Calhoun's income is below 400% of the applicable federal poverty level.
D. Calhoun is currently unemployed and receiving only unemployment compensation.

85. Desiree owes $900 in income taxes for 2022. She doesn't have the funds to pay the entire amount all at once. She plans to file her tax return on time, but she would like to make monthly payments on the amount due. When does interest begin to accrue on the amount that she owes?

A. She will not owe any interest because the amount that she owes is less than the safe harbor threshold of $1,000.
B. Interest accrues on any unpaid tax from the due date of the return (not including extensions) until the date of payment in full.
C. Interest accrues on any unpaid tax from the due date of the return (including extensions) until the date of payment in full.
D. Interest begins to accrue on the amount due on the close of the tax year (December 31).

86. What information should a tax preparer review to deter the possibility of identity theft?

A. Photo identification.
B. Form W-2.
C. Last year's tax return.
D. Utility statement.

87. Can multiple preparers in one tax office share a single PTIN?

A. Yes.
B. Yes, but only at the same office location.
C. Yes, but only if the principal preparer continues to sign the tax returns.
D. No, each preparer must obtain his own PTIN.

88. Kareem's tax return was chosen for examination. He did not agree with the examiner's findings and wishes to appeal the examiner's conclusion. What must he do if he wants to request an appeal?

A. He has 30 days from the date of the examiner's decision letter to appeal.
B. He can file a claim with the U.S. Tax Court within 30 days of the examiner's decision letter.
C. He can submit an offer in compromise, requesting a review of the examiner's decision.
D. He can request a collection due process hearing within 30 days of the examiner's decision.

89. Sophie receives a notice of deficiency in the mail with respect to individual income tax. She fails to respond to the letter within 90 days. What is Sophie's option if she wants to contest her tax deficiency?

A. She can request an extension to the period of time for petitioning the U.S. Tax Court.
B. She cannot contest her tax deficiency in the U.S. Tax Court. She must pay the entire amount owed and submit a claim for a refund to the IRS. If denied, she can sue the IRS for a refund in a U.S. district court or Court of Federal Claims.
C. She cannot contest her tax in the U.S. Tax Court. She must pay a portion of the amount owed and submit a claim for a refund to the IRS. If denied, she can sue the IRS for a refund in a U.S. district court or Court of Federal Claims.
D. She has no more appeal rights and owes the tax deficiency.

90. Which of the following persons may represent a taxpayer at an IRS Appeals conference?

A. An unenrolled tax preparer who prepared the tax return in question.
B. An enrolled agent.
C. A friend of the taxpayer.
D. A disbarred practitioner with a current PTIN.

91. Karen is a full-time employee for Bridgeline Construction, Inc. She is the company bookkeeper and prepares all the payroll tax returns as well as the W-2 forms for the employees. During the year, Bridgeline Construction receives an IRS notice regarding a payroll tax issue. Karen is not an enrolled practitioner. Can Karen represent her employer before the IRS?

A. No, Karen may not represent her employer before the IRS.
B. Karen may respond to the notice, but a company officer must sign it.
C. Karen may only respond to the notice if the company president makes her a bona-fide officer of the company.
D. Karen may represent her employer before the IRS because she is a full-time employee of the business.

92. Dabir is a tax preparer working for a national tax franchise. He would like to become an electronic return originator (ERO), so he can start his own home-based tax practice and e-file his clients' returns. What is the first step he should take in this application process?

A. Create an IRS e-Services account.
B. Undergo a thorough background check of his tax compliance history.
C. Apply for a PTIN.
D. Apply for an electronic filing identification number (EFIN).

93. Solomon is an enrolled agent. He mailed an advertisement announcing a flat rate of $100 for the preparation of a tax return for new clients. Solomon gets inundated with calls, and wants to increase the price. Solomon is bound by this advertised rate for a minimum of _____ days after the last date on which the fee schedule was published.

A. 20 days.
B. 30 days.
C. 45 days.
D. 60 days.

94. Omar is an enrolled agent. His client, Fatima, has a large tax deficiency. Fatima tells Omar she has no intention of paying her tax liability, no matter what, even though she has more than enough financial resources to easily pay the tax deficiency in full. Knowing that his client is not compliant, Omar advises Fatima to submit a request for a Collection Due Process hearing in order to stop collection activity. Is Omar in violation of Circular 230?

A. Yes, as the submission is only to delay tax administration.
B. No, since it gives Omar's client additional time to pay her tax liability.
C. No, since Omar cannot control his client's actions and is simply giving advice regarding her legal options.
D. There is insufficient information to make a determination.

95. If the IRS declares a taxpayer to be in "currently not collectible" status, which of the following is true?

A. The IRS will not require or expect the taxpayer to make payments toward the liability.
B. Penalties and interest accruals will be suspended.
C. The IRS is prohibited from filing a notice of federal tax lien.
D. The collection statute of limitations is suspended.

96. Alexa owes $4,000 when she files her tax return. She is not able to pay the entire balance due by the due date of the return. What of the following is **not** an acceptable payment option?

A. Alexa can submit an Installment Agreement Request and pay in installments.
B. Alexa can make payments online at *www.pay.gov.*
C. Alexa can pay her IRS debt using her credit card.
D. Alexa can contest her liability in the U.S. Tax Court.

97. The Freedom of Information Act (FOIA) does not require the IRS to release all documents that are subject to FOIA requests. The IRS may withhold information:

A. Due to budget cuts.
B. Due to the statute of limitations for FOIA requests.
C. If the requester fails to provide notarized identification along with the request.
D. For an IRS record that falls under one of the FOIA's nine statutory exemptions, or by one of three exclusions under the Act.

98. Which of the following professional designations is always required to obtain a PTIN?

A. CPAs.
B. Attorneys.
C. Enrolled agents.
D. Certified Financial Planners.

99. Oliver has a large tax debt from a prior year, but in 2022, he sustains a serious injury and subsequently loses his job. He is experiencing serious financial hardship and cannot pay his normal living expenses. What status allows people in financial hardship situations to defer paying their tax bill until their situation improves?

A. Currently not collectible.
B. Permanently not collectible.
C. Typically uncollectible.
D. Financially bankrupt.

100. In the licensing of enrolled agents, an "enrollment cycle" refers to:

A. The enrollment year preceding the effective date of renewal.
B. The three successive enrollment years preceding the effective date of renewal.
C. The year in which the enrolled agent receives his initial enrollment.
D. The amount of continuing professional education required each year of enrollment.

Please review your answer choices with the correct answers in the next section.

Answers to Exam #2: Representation

1. The answer is B. In the case regarding complaints for the sanctioning of a practitioner, discovery may be permitted at the discretion of an Administrative Law Judge (References: Cir. 230, Sections 10.63(a), 10.70(a) and 10.71(a)). This question is based on a released EA exam question.

2. The answer is C. Luther may appeal the judge's decision to the Treasury Appellate Authority. A practitioner may appeal the decision to the Treasury Appellate Authority within 30 days after the decision. The IRS may also appeal the judge's decision, if a decision was reached in favor of the practitioner. In either case, the Treasury Appellate Authority will receive briefs and render what is known as the "Final Agency Decision." For the OPR, this decision is final, but the practitioner may contest the Final Agency Decision in U.S. district court. The judge will review the findings from the administrative law hearing but will only set aside the decision if it is considered arbitrary or capricious, contrary to law, or an abuse of discretion.

3. The answer is D. Generally, confidential taxpayer information can only be disclosed upon a taxpayer's written authorization. However, a tax return preparer is not required to obtain disclosure consent from a client if the disclosure is made for any of the following reasons:
- A court order or subpoena issued by any court of record whether at the federal, state, or local level. The required information must be clearly identified in the document (subpoena or court order) in order for a preparer to disclose information.
- An administrative order, demand, summons, or subpoena issued by any federal agency (such as the IRS), state agency, or commission charged under the laws of the state with licensing, registration, or regulation of tax return preparers.
- To report a crime to proper authorities. Even if the preparer is mistaken and no crime has occurred, he will not be subject to sanctions if he makes the disclosure in good faith.
- For purposes of peer reviews.
- Finally, a preparer may disclose private client information to his attorney, or to an employee of the IRS, in connection with an IRS investigation of the preparer.

4. The answer is C. Agustina cannot negotiate or cash a taxpayer's refund check, even if she has the client's permission to do so. All of the other actions would be permitted.

5. The answer is A. Under IRS e-file rules, a tax preparer is not allowed to electronically file a client's tax return using a pay stub only. The preparer must wait until the client has a Form W-2 (there are exceptions for taxpayers who require a substitute Form W-2, *Form 4852, Substitute for Form W-2, Wage and Tax Statement*) such as when an employer goes out of business, and the forms are never issued, but these instances are rare. A substitute W-2 form should only be used when all other avenues are exhausted, and the taxpayer cannot reasonably obtain a Form W-2 from the employer).

6. The answer is D. A Statutory Notice of Deficiency is also known as a 90-day letter because the taxpayer generally has 90 days from the date of the letter to file a petition with the United States Tax Court. The deadline increases to 150 days if the notice is addressed to a taxpayer who is outside the country.

7. The answer is B. All of Joey's actions, when seen as a whole, indicate fraud. Fraud, as distinguished from negligence, is always intentional. One of the elements of fraud is the intent to evade tax. The existence of several "badges of fraud" will usually indicate fraud, rather than negligence.

8. The answer is C. A financial account or prepaid debit card can have a maximum of <u>three refunds</u> direct deposited into it per tax year. Any additional deposits for the year for which an electronic refund is requested will be converted to a paper refund check and mailed to the taxpayer. The IRS is limiting the number to try to prevent criminals from easily obtaining multiple refunds.

9. The answer is D. Interest owed by a taxpayer will be abated or waived in the following instances:

- When it is excessive, barred by statute, or erroneously or illegally assessed.
- When it is assessed on an erroneous refund.
- When it was incurred while the taxpayer was in a combat zone or in a declared disaster area.

Further, the IRS will waive interest that is the result of certain errors or delays caused by an IRS employee, which are known as managerial acts and ministerial acts. However, (in contrast to abatement of penalties, which can be abated for reasonable cause), reasonable cause is not allowed as the basis for abatement of interest.

10. The answer is C. Only valid SSA documents such as Social Security cards should be used to confirm the validity of a taxpayer's Social Security number and name spelling. A driver's license or passport should not be used in lieu of SSA records.

11. The answer is B. Trent's IRS interview must be suspended when he clearly requests to consult with a representative. Throughout the examination process, a taxpayer can act on his own behalf or have someone represent him. The taxpayer is not required to be present if the representative is a federally authorized practitioner (generally, an enrolled agent, CPA, or attorney). The taxpayer is also not required to be present if the representative is one of the other qualified individuals listed in Circular 230, such as a family member, an employee representing an employer, or an unenrolled preparer who is authorized to represent the taxpayer (with more limited rights than enrolled representatives) because he has prepared the return under examination and has completed all of the Annual Filing Season Program requirements.

12. The answer is C. The IRS cannot issue refunds before February 15, for returns that claim the Earned Income Tax Credit (EITC) and/or the Additional Child Tax Credit (ACTC). This delay applies to the entire refund, not just the portion associated with these credits. The delay applies to all methods of tax filing, whether the taxpayer uses a return preparer, or prepares the tax return themselves. Taxpayers who file their returns after February 15 will not be impacted. Refunds based only on over-withholding or any other tax credits will not be held.[6]

13. The answer is A. To claim the Earned Income Tax Credit, the taxpayer (and spouse, if filing a joint return) must have a valid Social Security number. The SSN must also be valid for employment purposes. Any qualifying child listed on Schedule EIC also must have a valid SSN (unless the child was born and died in the same year).

14. The answer is C. Safeguarding of IRS e-file from fraud and abuse is the shared responsibility of the IRS and Authorized IRS e-file Providers (see Publication 1345 for more information).

15. The answer is C. For remote interactions, Patrick must verify that the name, Social Security number, address, date of birth, and other personal information provided by the taxpayer are consistent with information obtained through record checks with applicable agencies or institutions, or through credit bureaus or similar databases. In an effort to cut down on identity theft, the IRS has instituted new measures for tax preparers who accept electronic signatures to authenticate the identity of taxpayers. The procedures vary depending on whether the tax preparer's interaction with the taxpayer is in person or remote. For in-person interactions, the preparer must inspect a valid government-issued picture ID, compare the picture to the applicant, and record the name, Social Security number, address, and date of birth, unless the preparer has identified the same client in the past using these procedures while originating the client's tax return. A credit check or other identity verification is optional.

16. The answer is B. IRC section 7525 grants a limited confidentiality privilege to enrolled practitioners. This confidentiality privilege does not extend to the mere preparation of income tax returns. Therefore, any of Clarence's discussions surrounding the preparation of a tax return are not privileged. The privilege under section 7525 may only be asserted in non-criminal tax matters before the IRS and non-criminal tax proceedings in federal court actions. Only a licensed attorney would have privilege in criminal tax proceedings.

17. The answer is C. An Individual Taxpayer Identification Number (ITIN) is a tax processing number issued by the Internal Revenue Service. Due to new procedures, ITINs will automatically expire after three years of nonuse.

---

[6] The Protecting Americans from Tax Hikes (PATH) Act stipulates that the IRS must withhold refunds for filers who claim these tax credits until February 15.

18. The answer is A. Receipt of taxpayer refund checks is allowed, but the tax practitioner must have a power of attorney to do so. A practitioner may never cash (or endorse) a taxpayer refund check. A power of attorney is not required in some situations when dealing with the IRS. The following situations do not require a power of attorney:

- Providing information to the IRS.
- Disclosure of tax return information based on authorization through Form 8821.
- Allowing the IRS to discuss return information with a third-party designee.
- Allowing the IRS to discuss return information with a fiduciary.
- Representing a taxpayer through a non-written (oral) consent.

19. The answer is D. A summons cannot require a taxpayer or a witness to prepare or create documents, including tax returns. A summons also cannot be issued solely to harass a taxpayer or to pressure him into settling a dispute. The IRS has broad legal authority to issue a summons when a taxpayer or other witness refuses to comply with requests for IRS records or other information. IRC section 7602 authorizes the IRS to issue summonses for the following purposes:

- To ascertain the correctness of any return,
- To prepare a return where none has been made,
- To determine the liability of a person for internal revenue tax,
- To determine the liability at law or in equity of a transferee or fiduciary of a person in respect to any internal revenue tax,
- To collect any internal revenue tax liability, or
- To inquire into any civil or criminal offense connected with the administration or enforcement of the internal revenue law.

A summons should require only that the witness appear on a given date to provide testimony or produce existing books, paper, and records that "may be relevant or material."

20. The answer is D. The primary tax authority is the Internal Revenue Code (IRC), which is enforced by the Internal Revenue Service (IRS). The second highest authority next to the Internal Revenue Code is Treasury Department Regulations. Treasury Department Regulations have the full force and effect of the law. The next highest authority would be Revenue Rulings, which are issued by the IRS' National Office. Revenue Rulings are public administrative rulings by the Internal Revenue Service (IRS) that apply the law to particular factual situations. A Revenue Ruling does not have the force of law, but it can be relied upon as precedent by all taxpayers. A private letter ruling, or PLR, is a written statement issued to a taxpayer that interprets and applies tax laws only to the taxpayer's represented set of facts. A private letter ruling binds only the IRS and the requesting taxpayer. Thus, a private ruling may not be cited or relied upon for precedent. However, a private letter ruling (PLR) can provide interpretation and application of law and regulation with respect to a taxpayer and are often used as a source of guidance.

21. The answer is C. A practitioner must submit records or information requested by the IRS unless the practitioner believes that the records or information are privileged.

22. The answer is A. Enrolled agents, like attorneys and certified public accountants (CPAs), have unlimited practice rights before the IRS. This means they are unrestricted as to which taxpayers they can represent, what types of tax matters they can handle, and the IRS offices they can practice before. They do not have rights before the U.S. Tax Court (unless having passed a special exam and meeting other U.S. Tax Court requirements) or other U.S. courts.

23. The answer is D. The IRS may accept an offer in compromise based on three grounds: (a) doubt as to collectibility, (b) effective tax administration, or (c) doubt as to liability.

24. The answer is D. Beverly may file a second claim. If a taxpayer's Innocent Spouse Claim was previously denied and now the taxpayer has new additional information, she can file a second claim, provide the new additional information, and it will be reconsidered by the IRS. However, she will normally not have the right to appeal to the U.S. Tax Court rights on this second reconsideration.

25. The answer is A. A practitioner may not charge a separate fee for direct deposit. Charging a flat fee for e-filing is allowed. However, some individual states, such as New York, mandate e-filing of all tax returns, and do not permit practitioners to charge a separate fee for e-filing.

26. The answer is C. Rosalee may qualify for injured spouse relief by filing to receive her share of the refund that was applied toward her husband's debt. Injured spouse relief may also apply when a spouse has past-due income tax, child support, or other obligations that are applied toward a tax refund.

> **Note:** An *injured* spouse is not to be confused with an *innocent* spouse, which is a different legal situation. If certain conditions are met, an innocent spouse may apply for relief from additional tax if a spouse or former spouse failed to report income or claimed improper deductions on a jointly filed tax return.

27. The answer is D. An offer in compromise (OIC) is an agreement between the taxpayer and the government that settles a tax liability (a tax deficiency, plus penalties and interest) for payment of less than the full amount owed (based on a released EA exam question).

28. The answer is B. If a CPA is suspended from practice by a state board of accountancy, the practitioner may also be disbarred from practice before the IRS, regardless of whether the suspension was due to a nontax matter.

29. The answer is C. When applying to become an authorized IRS e-services provider, an individual who is certified or licensed (such as an attorney, CPA, or enrolled agent) must enter current professional status information. All other individuals, including unenrolled tax return preparers, must be fingerprinted as part of the application process.

30. The answer is A. Betty is allowed to destroy the records related to her continuing professional education four years following the date of the EA renewal for which the CE is credited.

31. The answer is D. Griffin may qualify for equitable relief. Unlike "innocent spouse" relief or "separation of liability" relief, if a taxpayer qualifies for equitable relief, the taxpayer can get relief from an understatement of tax or an underpayment of tax. "Equitable relief" is only available if the taxpayer meets all of the following conditions:
- He or she does not qualify for innocent spouse relief or the separation of liability election.
- The IRS determines that it is unfair to hold the taxpayer liable for the understatement of tax, taking into account all the facts and circumstances.

32. The answer is C. Any individual who is paid a fee to prepare a return must sign it and fill out the preparer area of the return. This is true even when the paying client is a family member. An employee working for an employer may not have to sign the return if the employer has the ultimate liability for the return's accuracy.

33. The answer is B. In most cases, tax returns are audited for up to three years after filing. However, the IRS may audit for up to six years if there is substantial unreported income. An understatement of more than 25% of the gross income listed on the return is considered a "substantial understatement." There is no statute of limitations for a fraudulent return.

34. The answer is D. An IRS power of attorney is valid until revoked (or withdrawn). It may be revoked by the taxpayer or withdrawn by the representative, or it may be superseded by the filing of a new power of attorney for the same tax and tax period. An IRS power of attorney also terminates automatically upon the taxpayer's death or incompetency.

35. The answer is B. A tax preparer who violates due diligence requirements faces a $560 penalty for each violation in 2023 (for 2022 tax year returns being prepared). This penalty is now adjusted for inflation each year.

36. The answer is C. Sylvie must turn the check directly over to William. A tax preparer must not endorse or otherwise cash any refund check issued to the taxpayer. A preparer cannot withhold a taxpayer's refund check because of a fee dispute. However, a preparer is not required to file a client's tax return without first obtaining payment.

37. The answer is D. The Revenue Agent must advise Jeronimo that he has a right to refuse to extend the statute of limitations and if he does agree to an extension, the agreement can be restricted as to particular issues on the tax return. Taxpayers are not required to extend the limitations period.

38. The answer is B. When an individual strikes out the jurat on a return, it becomes a frivolous return. The jurat is an affidavit in which the taxpayer and/or preparer attests to the truth of the information contained on the return and attached return information. The jurat is signed under penalty of perjury.

Alteration of the jurat is prohibited and will result in a frivolous return.

Sign Here	Under penalties of perjury, I declare that I have examined this return and accompanying schedules and statements, and to the best of my knowledge and belief, they are true, correct, and complete. Declaration of preparer (other than taxpayer) is based on all information of which preparer has any knowledge.				
Joint return? See instructions. Keep a copy for your records.	Your signature	Date	Your occupation		If the IRS sent you an Identity Protection PIN, enter it here (see inst.)
	Spouse's signature. If a joint return, **both** must sign.	Date	Spouse's occupation		If the IRS sent you an Identity Protection PIN, enter it here (see inst.)
Paid Preparer Use Only	Preparer's name	Preparer's signature		PTIN	Firm's EIN	Check if: ☐ 3rd Party Designee
	Firm's name ▶			Phone no.		☐ Self-employed
	Firm's address ▶					

39. The answer is B. A formal complaint against a practitioner may be served in the following ways: certified mail; first-class mail; if previously returned undelivered, by certified mail; private delivery service; in person; or by leaving the complaint at the office of the practitioner. Electronic delivery, such as e-mail, is not a valid means of serving a complaint.

40. The answer is A. Rachel will be an enrolled agent when she is issued her enrollment card. An enrolled agent becomes official on the date the Return Preparer Office issues their enrollment card. Form 23 is only the application for enrollment. An applicant must undergo a background check prior to enrollment. It can take up to 60 days or more for the IRS to process an application.

41. The answer is C. A practitioner is not allowed to charge an "unconscionable fee" for his services. Circular 230 prohibits a practitioner from charging an unconscionable fee in the preparation of a tax return or other engagement. "Unconscionable fees" are not defined in Circular 230. The other choices are acceptable fee practices.

42. The answer is C. The penalty assessed against Tasha will be 75% of the underpayment due to fraud. This 75% penalty applies only in the circumstances of civil fraud.

43. The answer is D. Circular 230 states that a practitioner may not willfully sign a tax return or claim for refund that the practitioner knows (or reasonably should know) contains a position that:

- Lacks a reasonable basis;
- Is an unreasonable position, or;
- Is a willful attempt by the practitioner to understate the liability for tax, or reckless or intentional disregard of rules or regulations.

44. The answer is C. Performance as a notary is not considered disreputable conduct. A practitioner may perform duties as a notary public. However, a practitioner who is a notary public and is engaged in a matter before the IRS (or who has a material interest in the matter) cannot engage in any notary activities related to that matter. All of the other acts listed are considered disreputable conduct. The definition of "disreputable conduct" includes:

- Willfully failing to e-file returns electronically if they fall under the e-filing mandate, and
- Failing to include a valid PTIN on tax returns.

45. The answer is A. Dottie must attach Form 8275, *Disclosure Statement,* to disclose a tax position on a tax return. Taxpayers and tax preparers may use this form (or Form 8275-R if a position taken on a return runs contrary to Treasury regulations) to disclose items or positions on a tax return in order to avoid certain penalties.

46. The answer is B. A paper copy is not required. The preparer must provide a complete copy of the return to the taxpayer. Preparers may provide this copy using any media, including electronic, that is acceptable to both the taxpayer and the preparer. The client's copy must include the preparer's PTIN.

47. The answer is D. Suzanne must ask her client additional questions if the information furnished seems incorrect or incomplete. Under tax preparer due diligence requirements, a preparer must not know (or have reason to know) that the information used to determine eligibility for the AOTC, the EITC, or the CTC/ACTC is incorrect.

48. The answer is A. Amanda is required to have both a PTIN and an EFIN. Each tax preparer needs to have her own PTIN, which is issued to individuals. An electronic filing identification number (EFIN) is a number issued by the IRS to individuals or firms that have been approved as authorized IRS e-file providers. All preparers in a firm may be covered by a single EFIN.

> **Note:** Specified tax return preparers without social security numbers who are foreign persons living and working abroad are exempt from the requirement to e-file if they are not members of a firm that is eligible to e-file. In this scenario, a foreign preparer would be exempt from the e-file mandate, but would still be required to have a PTIN.

49. The answer is D. A private letter ruling (PLR) is a written communication from the Internal Revenue Service in response to a taxpayer's written request for guidance on a particular tax issue. PLRs become public record once issued, and all of the taxpayer's personal information is removed. Private Letter Rulings are not free. The cost of many Private Letter Rulings can be $38,000, with some costing less and a few costing even more. A PLR is specific to a particular taxpayer's situation and may not be an acceptable authority for any other taxpayer, however, PLRs are a source of valuable information for tax professionals and taxpayers alike.

50. The answer is C. The U.S. Tax Court has a simplified procedure for taxpayers whose amount in dispute, including applicable penalties, is $50,000 or less (per tax year). If the amount of the dispute is $50,000 or less, taxpayers may choose to use the Tax Court small tax case procedure. Trials in small tax cases are less formal. However, decisions entered pursuant to small tax case procedures are not appealable.

> **Note:** Do not confuse the U.S. Tax Court's "Small Case Procedure" with the IRS' "Small Case Request." They are not the same thing. A "Small Case Request" is a procedure within the IRS appeals division (not with the U.S. Tax Court). A taxpayer who is going through the IRS appeals process may submit a Small Case Request if the entire amount of additional tax and penalties proposed for each tax year is $25,000 or less.

51. The answer is B. There are three types of Treasury regulations: legislative, interpretive, and procedural. There is no such thing as a "Congressional regulation" issued by the Treasury Department.

52. The answer is C. Josiah must promptly advise his client of the consequences of any noncompliance, error, or omission. He is not required to notify the IRS of the noncompliance.

53. The answer is A. IRS examiners are instructed to work out times, dates, and locations that are convenient for the taxpayer. A taxpayer may request a change of venue as a matter of convenience (for example, if the taxpayer moved from California to New Jersey and his tax preparer is still living in California). However, the IRS has the right to make all final decisions regarding the timing and location of an audit.

54. The answer is B. A third-party designee may respond to IRS notices about math errors, offsets, and return preparation. The taxpayer completes the Third-Party Designee Authorization directly on the tax return, entering the designee's name and phone number and a self-selected five-digit PIN, which the designee will have to confirm when requesting information from the IRS. A third-party designee may:

- Exchange information concerning the return with the IRS,
- Call the IRS for information about the processing of the return or the status of refund or payments; and
- Respond to certain IRS notices about math errors, offsets, and return preparation.

The taxpayer cannot use the third-party designee to authorize a practitioner to receive a tax refund check, bind the taxpayer to any IRS contract or agreement (including additional tax liability), or otherwise represent the taxpayer before the IRS.

55. The answer is D. Alexander must only attach Form 8938, Statement of Specified Foreign Financial Assets, to his federal return. The FBAR (Form 114, Report of Foreign Bank and Financial Accounts) is not filed with the IRS. It must be filed online with the Financial Crimes Enforcement Network e-filing system.

56. The answer is A. Renata's client cannot designate his direct deposit to a credit card account. Taxpayers often elect the direct deposit option because it is the fastest way of receiving refunds. Providers must accept a direct deposit election to any eligible financial institution designated by the taxpayer. The taxpayer may designate refunds to savings, checking, share draft, prepaid debit card, or consumer asset accounts (for example, IRA or money market accounts).

57. The answer is D. The centralized authorization file (CAF) is the IRS' computer database that contains information regarding the authorizations that taxpayers have given representatives for their accounts. When either a Form 2848, *Power of Attorney or Declaration of Representation*, or Form 8821, *Tax Information Authorization*, is submitted to the IRS, it is processed for inclusion in the CAF, and a CAF number is assigned to the tax practitioner or another authorized individual.

58. The answer is B. The Annual Filing Season Program is a *voluntary program*. Return preparers who complete the requirements for the Annual Filing Season Program will be issued a Record of Completion that they can display and use to differentiate themselves in the marketplace if desired. The IRS encourages non-credentialed tax return preparers to participate. Completing the AFSP also allows a non-enrolled preparer to represent a taxpayer, with limitations, in an audit of a return that the practitioner prepared.

59. The answer is D. Stacy must inform each client of the potential for conflict of interest and then obtain written waivers of the conflict from both clients. Circular 230 requires a practitioner to notify each client of the conflict and have each client provide informed consent, confirmed in writing. The consent must be signed no later than 30 days after the conflict is known by the practitioner and it must be retained for 36 months. When a conflict of interest exists, a practitioner must reasonably believe that she will be able to provide competent and diligent representation to each client.

60. The answer is B. Edward has 30 days to respond. If an IRS examiner determines a section 6694 penalty applies:

- A detailed report is prepared.
- The preparer is provided with a copy.
- The preparer then has 30 days to request an appeal before the penalty is assessed.

Section 6694 penalties are due to understatements of taxpayer's liability, and they apply to tax preparers (not the actual client themselves). There are two types of Section 6694 penalties.

- **IRC §6694(a):** An understatement due to an unreasonable position: This penalty is the greater of $1,000 or 50% of the income derived by the tax return preparer with respect to the return.
- **IRC §6694(b):** An understatement due to willful or reckless conduct: This penalty is the greater of $5,000 or 75% of the income derived by the tax return preparer with respect to the return or claim for refund.

61. The answer is C. A "remote transaction" for electronic signature is one in which the taxpayer is electronically signing the signature authorization form, and the ERO is not physically present with the taxpayer. For remote transactions, the ERO must record the taxpayer's name, social security number, address and date of birth.

62. The answer is B. A significant and unexpected tax liability is not a sufficient reason to receive help from the Taxpayer Advocate Service (TAS). The TAS is a free and confidential service within the IRS whose goal is to help taxpayers resolve problems with other IRS divisions. Situations where the TAS may offer assistance include the following:

- The taxpayer will suffer significant costs if relief is not granted.
- The taxpayer has experienced a delay of more than 30 days to resolve a tax issue.
- The taxpayer did not receive a response or resolution to his problem or inquiry by the date promised.
- A system or procedure has either failed to operate as intended, or failed to resolve the taxpayer's problem or dispute within the IRS, or
- The manner in which the tax laws are being administered raises considerations of equity, or it has impaired or will impair the taxpayer's rights.

63. The answer is B. Natalie is required to take a minimum of 16 hours per year, two of which must be on ethics. In addition to this annual minimum requirement, enrolled agents must obtain 72 hours of continuing education every three years. For renewal purposes, the annual CPE requirements only apply for the years during which someone was an enrolled agent.

> **Note:** An EA who receives initial enrollment during an enrollment cycle must complete two CE hours for each month enrolled during the enrollment cycle. Enrollment for any part of a month is considered enrollment for the entire month. In addition, an EA who receives their initial enrollment during an enrollment cycle must complete two CE hours of ethics or professional conduct for each year enrolled during the enrollment cycle.

64. The answer is A. Rejected electronic individual income tax return data can be corrected and retransmitted without new signatures or authorizations if changes do not differ from the amounts of "total income" or "AGI" on the original electronic return by more than $50, or from the amounts of "total tax", "federal income tax withheld", "refund" or "amount you owe" by more than $14. However, the preparer must give the taxpayer a copy of the corrected tax return.

65. The answer is A. Paul and Donatella can use Form 8888 to split their refund any way they wish. In most cases, tax refunds can be split using direct deposit in up to three separate accounts (such as a checking account, savings account, mutual fund account, or credit union account), as long as the account is located in the United States. Deposits cannot be made into foreign bank accounts.

66. The answer is C. The IP PIN is not used in place of a taxpayer's signature. The IP PIN is a 6-digit number assigned to eligible taxpayers to help prevent the misuse of their Social Security number on fraudulent federal income tax returns. The IP PIN helps the IRS verify a taxpayer's identity and accept their electronic or paper tax return.

67. The answer is D. When the IRS rejects a return that an Electronic Return Originator (ERO) attempted to e-file for a taxpayer, the ERO must advise the taxpayer of the rejection and provide the taxpayer with the reject code (also called "business rules" or "BR"), accompanied by an explanation (see IRS Publication 1345, *Handbook for Authorized IRS e file Providers).*

68. The answer is D. The OPR can issue a notice for judicial proceedings for censure, suspension, or disbarment. It can also send a letter of reprimand to a preparer. Criminal penalties may be imposed on a tax preparer for fraudulent activity, but the OPR refers criminal activity to the IRS's own criminal division or to the Department of Justice for potential prosecution.

69. The answer is C. A tax refund cannot be used to purchase municipal bonds directly (only U.S. Savings Bonds). Taxpayers have a number of options related to their tax refunds. They may:

- Apply a refund to next year's estimated tax.
- Receive the refund as a direct deposit.
- Receive the refund as a paper check.
- Split the refund, with a portion applied to next year's estimated tax and the remainder received as direct deposit or a paper check.
- Use the refund (or part of it) to purchase U.S. Series I Savings Bonds. Taxpayers can purchase up to $5,000 in bonds for themselves or others.

70. The answer is C. The U.S. Tax Court lacks jurisdiction over FBAR penalty matters. The jurisdiction of the Tax Court includes:

- Income tax, estate tax, and gift tax.
- Worker classification.
- Innocent spouse claims.
- Liens and levies.
- Awards of administrative costs.
- Redetermination of interest.
- Modification of estate tax decisions.
- Litigation costs awards.
- Abatement of interest.

71. The answer is B. A taxpayer who files a tax return that is considered "frivolous" faces a potential penalty of $5,000, in addition to any other penalty provided by law. This penalty may be doubled on a joint return. A taxpayer will be subject to this penalty if he files a tax return based simply on the desire to interfere with the administration of tax law. The penalty for making frivolous arguments before the U.S. Tax Court is even steeper at $25,000.

72. The answer is A. Callum may represent his daughter before the IRS if Genie signs a Form 2848, because she is a member of his immediate family. Immediate family means a spouse, child, parent, grandparent, grandchild, brother, or sister of the individual. For the purposes of this rule, stepparents, stepchildren, stepbrothers, and stepsisters are also considered immediate family as well. Because of their special relationship, immediate family members can represent a taxpayer and practice before the IRS, provided they present satisfactory identification and proof of authority to do so. In this case, Callum would need a signed Form 2848 with Genie's signature.

73. The answer is B. Penny may appeal the termination of her installment agreement. If she appeals within a 30-day period after the termination, the IRS will be prohibited from levying her assets until her appeal is completed.

74. The answer is B. For individuals without a valid SSN; a tax professional should explain that they must have a taxpayer identification number. If the taxpayer has an existing ITIN, the tax professional should request a copy of the ITIN card or letter. If a taxpayer does not have an ITIN but needs to request one, an ITIN can be requested by filing Form W-7, *Application for IRS Individual Taxpayer Identification Number (ITIN)*, with the taxpayer's federal income tax return.

75. The answer is D. The date of filing is not required. However, it is necessary to state the year or periods involved, such as "2019-2023 tax years." An IRS power of attorney must contain:

- The type of tax and the tax years covered.
- The name and address of the representative.
- The name and taxpayer identification (number of the taxpayer).
- The signatures of the representative and the taxpayer.

The IRS will not accept a power of attorney if it does not contain all the information listed above.

76. The answer is C. Under regulations pertaining to IRC section 6662, sources of "substantial authority" of federal tax law include the following: provisions of the Internal Revenue Code, temporary and final regulations, court cases, administrative pronouncements, tax treaties, and Congressional intent as reflected in official congressional committee reports. This list was later expanded to include proposed regulations, private letter rulings, technical advice memoranda, IRS information or press releases, notices, and any other similar documents published by the IRS in the Internal Revenue Bulletin. The information in IRS publications is drawn from the Internal Revenue Code, Treasury regulations, and other primary sources of authority, but IRS publications themselves are not considered to have substantial authority. The same is true for IRS tax forms and instructions. The Internal Revenue Manual is essentially a policy and operations manual for IRS employees. It is an official compilation of policies, delegated authorities, procedures, instructions, and guidelines relating to the organization, functions, administration, and operations of the IRS, but it does not itself have substantial authority.

77. The answer is A. Under Circular 230, the definition of a tax return includes the following: an original return, an amended return, or a claim for a refund.

78. The answer is B. Chandler has five days to file the return on paper, and mail it to the IRS. The return will still be considered timely-filed. When re-submitting a previously-rejected return as a paper return, the taxpayer must file the return (1) by the due date for filing the return or (2) within 5 calendar days after the return was rejected. Individual tax returns have a "perfection period" of 5 days from the date of rejection, while most business returns have a "perfection period" of 10 days from the date of rejection.

79. The answer is D. An individual who provides only typing, reproduction or other mechanical assistance in the preparation of a return is not a tax return preparer and is not under the jurisdiction of Circular 230. Because she is not a paid preparer, she also would not be required to obtain a PTIN. The following are subject to Circular 230 jurisdiction, and thus to disciplinary oversight by the Office of Professional Responsibility:

- State licensed attorneys and CPAs who interact with federal tax administration at any level and capacity.

- Enrolled agents, enrolled retirement plan agents, and enrolled actuaries.

- Persons providing appraisals used in connection with tax matters (such as valuing estate and gift assets).

- Unlicensed individuals who represent taxpayers before the IRS examination division, IRS customer service, and Taxpayer Advocate Service in connection with returns they prepared and signed.

- Licensed and unlicensed individuals who give written advice that has the potential for tax avoidance or evasion.

- Any person submitting a power of attorney in connection with limited representation or special authorization to practice before the IRS in a specific matter before the agency.

80. The answer is B. Under Circular 230, a practitioner may not notarize documents for the clients he represents before the IRS. If the practitioner is a notary public and is employed as counsel, attorney, or agent in a matter before the IRS or has a material interest in the matter, he cannot engage in any notary activities relative to that matter. Answer "A" is incorrect, because practitioners are allowed to charge contingent fees in certain cases. Answer "C" is incorrect because a practitioner may represent clients with a conflict of interest as long as it is disclosed in writing to all affected parties and all parties agree in writing. Answer "D" is incorrect, because a practitioner may discuss and recommend tax shelters to a client. Not all tax shelters are abusive tax shelters, but the disclosure and ethics rules regarding tax shelters and tax shelter opinions are very strict.

81. The answer is A. Isadore is not an enrolled agent, CPA, or attorney, so she cannot represent Carlsbad Engineering in the examination of its prior-year returns. As an AFSP certificate holder, she could represent the company for its 2022 Form 1120-S only, which is the only return that she prepared.

82. The answer is D. Accounting students would be required to take the AFTR course in order to obtain a Record of Completion. Some unenrolled preparers are exempt from the AFTR course requirement because of their completion of other recognized state or national competency tests. These exempt groups are still required to meet other program requirements, including the CPE requirements. Return preparers who can obtain a Record of Completion without taking the AFTR course are:

- Anyone who passed the (now retired) Registered Tax Return Preparer exam.

- State-based return preparer program participants currently with testing requirements: Return preparers who are active registrants of the Oregon Board of Tax Practitioners, California Tax Education Council, or Maryland State Board of Individual Tax Preparers.

- Tax practitioners who have passed the Special Enrollment Exam Part I within the past two years.

- VITA volunteers (quality reviewers and instructors with active PTINs).

- Other accredited tax-focused credential-holders: The Accreditation Council for Accountancy and Taxation's Accredited Business Accountant (ABA) and Accredited Tax Preparer (ATP) programs.

- Enrolled practitioners are also exempt (EAs, CPAs, and attorneys).

83. The answer is D. Sterling cannot prepare or sign a tax return if he lacks sufficient competence. Competence requires the appropriate level of knowledge, skill, thoroughness, and preparation. Circular 230 states that competence can be achieved by consulting with experts in the relevant area or by studying the relevant law.

84. The answer is B. Taxpayers are generally charged a one-time fee to set up an installment agreement with the IRS. User fees may be reduced or waived entirely for low-income taxpayers who meet certain income thresholds. The IRS would waive the user fees for Calhoun's installment agreement request if Calhoun's income is at or below 250% of the applicable federal poverty level and he agreed to make electronic debit payments by entering into a Direct Debit Installment Agreement (DDIA) with the IRS. If a taxpayer is unable to make electronic debit payments by entering into a DDIA, they will be reimbursed the user fee upon the completion of the installment agreement.

85. The answer is B. Generally, interest accrues on any unpaid tax from the due date of the return (not including extensions) until the date of payment in full. This means that interest on any amounts due will begin to accrue after the filing deadline (April 18, 2023, is the filing deadline for 2022 returns). However, as long as Desiree files her return on time, she will not be assessed a failure-to-file penalty.

86. The answer is A. A tax practitioner should review a taxpayer's identification in order to help deter identity theft. Acceptable identification includes: a U.S. driver's license, passport, or other government-issued identification (this question is modified from the official IRS VITA training guide).

87. The answer is D. A PTIN cannot be shared. A PTIN is an individual preparer's number, so each preparer must obtain his own PTIN.

88. The answer is A. Kareem can request an appeal by mailing in a formal written protest within the time limit specified in the examiner's decision letter. The time limit is generally 30 days from the date of the letter. If Kareem does not respond to the 30-day letter, or if he later does not reach an agreement with an Appeals Officer, the IRS will send him a 90-day letter, at which point Kareem would be able to file a petition with the U.S. Tax Court.

89. The answer is B. Since Sophie failed to respond to the 90-day-letter, Sophie cannot contest her tax deficiency in the U.S. Tax Court. She must pay the amount owed and sue the IRS for a refund in a U.S. district court or Court of Federal Claims. A Notice of Deficiency (90-day letter) must be issued before a taxpayer can go to the Tax Court. Once the notice is issued, a taxpayer has 90 days from the date of the notice to respond and file a petition with the court. If a taxpayer fails to respond to the notice, she must pay the tax deficiency first and then sue the IRS for a refund in a U.S. district court or Court of Federal Claims.

90. The answer is B. Only a practitioner (generally, an enrolled agent, CPA, or tax attorney) with a signed power of attorney may represent a taxpayer at an IRS appeals conference. An unenrolled tax preparer may be a witness for a taxpayer at an appeals conference but may not serve as a representative for the taxpayer. An unenrolled tax preparer may represent a taxpayer before IRS revenue agents, but not before revenue officers or appeals officers. Only unenrolled return preparers participating in the Annual Filing Season Record of Completion (AFSP) program may represent a taxpayer, only with respect to returns prepared and signed by the preparer, and only in limited situations.

91. The answer is D. Karen may represent her employer before the IRS because she is a full-time employee of the business. In Circular 230 §10.7(c)(1), a regular full-time employee of a business may represent her employer before the IRS without being an enrolled practitioner.

92. The answer is A. Dabir must first create an IRS e-Services account. He will need to supply personal information, including his Social Security number or other taxpayer identification number and his address where the IRS will mail confirmation of the account. This part of the application process can take up to 45 days. After the IRS approves his e-Services account, Dabir will undergo a thorough IRS suitability check that may include a review of his criminal background, credit history, and tax compliance history. Only then will he be accepted as an authorized IRS e-file provider, an umbrella term for anyone authorized to participate in e-file, from software developers to transmitters. Preparers who want to e-file for clients must first be approved as electronic return originators (ERO). The application to become an authorized e-file provider must also identify a firm's principals and at least one responsible official.

93. The answer is B. A practitioner may publish and advertise a fee schedule. Solomon must adhere to the published fee schedule for at least 30 calendar days after it is published.

94. The answer is A. Omar is in violation of section 10.23 of Circular 230, which states that a practitioner must not unreasonably delay the prompt disposition of any matter before the IRS. Omar's advice is an example of making a submission to delay or impede tax administration, because the IRS will not consider the resolution of a collection action when a taxpayer is not in compliance.

95. The answer is A. "Currently-not-collectible" (or CNC) status means the IRS has determined that a taxpayer has no ability to pay his tax debts and that other options, such as an installment agreement or offer in compromise, are not feasible. While a taxpayer is in this status, generally all collection activities will be halted for at least one year, or until his income increases. Penalties and interest will continue to be added to the tax debt during this period.

96. The answer is D. Alexa cannot file a petition in the U.S. Tax Court to contest a valid tax liability. The Tax Court is a court of limited jurisdiction. The other choices are all valid payment methods for paying one's tax liability.

97. The answer is D. The IRS may withhold an IRS record that falls under one of the FOIA's nine statutory exemptions, or one of three exclusions under the Act. The exemptions protect against the disclosure of information that would harm the following: national security, the privacy of individuals, the proprietary interests of business, the functioning of the government, and other important recognized interests.

98. The answer is C. All Enrolled Agents are required to have a PTIN, even if they do not prepare any tax returns. Anyone who receives compensation for preparing all (or substantially all) of a federal tax return (or claim for refund), including attorneys and certified public accountants, is required to obtain a PTIN. CPAs and attorneys who do not prepare tax returns, such as a CPA who only does audit work or an attorney who only does criminal defense, do not need to obtain a PTIN. Certified Financial Planners are not required to obtain a PTIN if they do not prepare tax returns.

99. The answer is A. The Internal Revenue Service (IRS) is granted the authority to determine that some taxpayer accounts are CNC, or "currently not collectible." This status defers payment for taxpayers in financial hardship until their situation improves. The IRS' 10-year collection statute will continue to run during the time the taxpayer's account is in CNC status. CNC status is reviewed periodically by the IRS, to determine if the taxpayer still qualifies as "currently not collectible."

100. The answer is B. The enrollment cycle refers to the three successive enrollment years preceding the effective date of renewal.

#3 Sample Exam: Representation

(Please test yourself first, then check the correct answers at the end of this exam.)

1. What is a Notice of Federal Tax Lien?

A. A document filed with the local recording office that identifies tax liabilities owed by the taxpayer.
B. A filing that allows tax debt to be collected through a collection agency.
C. A statutory demand to ask for payment of a debt from an individual.
D. A petition filed by a debtor that begins the bankruptcy process.

2. Abella is a full-time bookkeeper for Ortega Brothers, LLC. As part of her job duties, she prepares the partnership return for Ortega Brothers, including Schedules K-1 for each of the individual partners. She does not prepare any other returns for compensation. Is Abella required to obtain a PTIN?

A. Yes, because she is considered a paid preparer and must obtain a PTIN.
B. No, she is not considered a paid preparer, and she is not required to obtain a PTIN.
C. Abella is allowed to forgo obtaining a PTIN only if the IRS provides her a written waiver.
D. Abella must request a PTIN, an EFIN and also submit to a background check.

3. Judith is an enrolled agent. In 2022, she fired a client for nonpayment. She had been representing the client in an IRS audit of their business. What action should Judith take with the IRS if she chooses to permanently end her representation of this particular client?

A. Nothing. It is the taxpayer's responsibility to notify the IRS.
B. She must call the IRS to revoke the POA.
C. She should formally withdraw from the engagement and write "WITHDRAW" across the top of Form 2848 and send it to the IRS via mail or fax.
D. She cannot withdraw from an audit engagement once the audit has already begun.

4. Circular 230 outlines expectations for written advice provided by a tax practitioner. Which of the following is a correct statement?

A. A practitioner can use the possibility of an IRS audit as a factor in providing the written advice.
B. A practitioner cannot use the possibility of an IRS audit as a factor in providing written advice.
C. Depending on the client's individual situation, a practitioner can use the possibility of an IRS audit as a factor in providing the written advice.
D. A practitioner can use the possibility of an IRS audit as a factor in providing the written advice for individual taxpayers but not for business entities.

5. Which of the following statements is *not* correct about becoming an enrolled agent?

A. All applicants must pass the three parts of the Special Enrollment Examination.
B. All applicants must pass a suitability check.
C. All applicants must be at least 18 years old.
D. All applicants must apply for enrollment by submitting Form 23.

6. Which of the following is not a requirement for participation in the Annual Filing Season Program?

A. The participant must have a valid PTIN.
B. The participant must consent to Circular 230.
C. The participant must have a valid EIN.
D. The participant must pass a suitability and tax compliance check.

7. Rory is a licensed notary public as well as an enrolled agent. Regarding Rory's notary commission, which of the following statements is correct?

A. A federally-authorized tax practitioner is not allowed to be a notary public.
B. A federally-authorized tax practitioner is required to be a notary public.
C. A federally-authorized tax practitioner cannot notarize any documents in which he has a material interest in matters before the IRS.
D. A federally-authorized tax practitioner can only notarize documents for clients if they sign a written consent.

8. If a taxpayer and the IRS fail to settle a non-docketed examination controversy in the IRS Appeals Office, the next event to occur is a/an:

A. Issuance of a notice of deficiency.
B. Issuance of notice and demand for payment.
C. Return of the case to the Revenue Agent for further review.
D. Referral of the case to the Taxpayer Advocate.

9. Mandy is self-employed, but she refuses to keep books and records. Instead, she simply estimates her income and expenses every year. Later, the IRS examines Mandy's most recent tax return and disallows the majority of the expenses. What penalty would the IRS be most likely to assess against Mandy?

A. An accuracy-related penalty of 20% of the underpayment of tax.
B. A fraud penalty of 75% for tax evasion.
C. A $5,000 penalty for filing a frivolous return.
D. A 25% penalty for failure-to-file a timely tax return.

10. Which of the following enrolled practitioners have the most limited area of practice before the IRS?

A. Enrolled agent.
B. Certified public accountant.
C. Attorney.
D. Enrolled actuary.

11. Enrolled agents are allowed to assert a limited practitioner confidentiality privilege relating to:

A. Noncriminal federal tax matters.
B. Noncriminal tax matters, including communications regarding tax shelters.
C. The preparation of tax returns.
D. Criminal and noncriminal tax matters brought before the IRS.

12. Aida is an enrolled agent who e-files an individual return for her client, Rolando. However, her client's e-filed return is rejected by the IRS just one day before the deadline. Aida cannot resolve the rejection issue, and the return must be filed on paper. In order to timely file the tax return, what is the deadline for filing a paper return?

A. The original due date of the return.
B. Five calendar days after the date the IRS first rejects the e-filed return.
C. Ten calendar days after the date that the IRS first rejects the return.
D. 30 calendar days after the date the IRS first rejected the return.

13. If an enrolled agent is disbarred from practice, the IRS will:

A. Allow the practitioner to represent clients before the IRS examination division.
B. Not recognize a power of attorney that names the individual as a representative.
C. Allow the enrolled agent to retain limited practice rights for representation of past clients.
D. None of the above.

14. On a jointly filed return (MFJ), both spouses are _____ for all the tax due, even if only one spouse earns any income.

A. Not responsible.
B. Independently liable.
C. Partially liable.
D. Jointly and severally liable.

15. Under Circular 230, a tax preparer is required to keep which of the following?

A. Copies of all tax returns prepared.
B. A list of clients and tax returns prepared that includes information about the taxpayer, tax year, and type of return prepared. The list may be stored electronically or kept as a hard copy.
C. Copies of all returns they have prepared or retain a list of clients, and the types of tax returns prepared.
D. Either a copy of all tax returns prepared, or a list of clients and tax returns prepared. However, hard copies are required in both cases. Electronic storage is acceptable, but is not by itself adequate and must be supplemented with hard copies of all required documents.

16. Which of the following persons could be an Electronic Return Originator (ERO)?

A. Tax attorney.
B. Volunteer Retirement Coordinator.
C. Certified Network Administrator.
D. Human Resources Specialist.

17. Which of the following may be grounds for denial of enrollment?

A. Failure to have a valid Social Security number.
B. Failure to have valid U.S. citizenship.
C. Failure to timely pay personal income taxes.
D. Personal bankruptcy.

18. For which refundable credit is a tax preparer *not* required to file Form 8867, *Paid Preparer's Due Diligence Checklist?*

A. Earned Income Credit.
B. Additional Child Tax Credit.
C. American Opportunity Tax Credit.
D. Credit for Excess Social Security and RRTA Tax Withheld.

19. Alma filed for personal bankruptcy during the year. She has an existing federal tax debt. What are the consequences in this scenario?

A. The collection statute of limitations is suspended by the length of time Alma is in bankruptcy, plus an additional six months.
B. A levy will be filed automatically against the taxpayer.
C. Delinquent returns will be filed on the taxpayer's behalf (SFR; substitute for return).
D. The filing of a Tax Court petition will be delayed.

20. What is required by every taxpayer who claims the Earned Income Tax Credit?

A. A qualifying dependent.
B. Physical presence in the U.S. for the entire tax year.
C. U.S. citizenship.
D. A valid Social Security number.

21. Reginald is an enrolled agent. He was disbarred from practice by the IRS for filing fraudulent returns. How many years must he wait before he can petition the IRS for reinstatement?

A. One year.
B. Five years.
C. Ten years.
D. Disbarment is permanent.

22. Esther is an enrolled agent. She has a former client named Kent, who she fired for nonpayment. During the year, Esther receives an IRS summons relating to Kent, with an order for her to appear before the IRS. What must Esther do about the summons?

A. Esther must respond to the summons.
B. Esther is not required to respond to the summons, but she must attempt to notify the IRS by mail that Kent is no longer her client.
C. Esther is required to forward the summons to Kent, but she is not required to respond to it since Kent is no longer her client.
D. Esther is not required to respond to the summons, nor is she required to notify her former client of the summons.

23. Once a taxpayer's tax liability is _____, the statute of limitations for collections begins to run.

A. Determined.
B. Assessed.
C. Estimated.
D. Levied.

24. With regards to federal taxes, the "statute of limitations for assessment" refers to what?

A. The maximum time period in which the IRS can assess a tax deficiency.
B. The maximum time period in which the IRS can charge a felony tax crime.
C. The maximum time period in which the IRS can disbar a tax practitioner.
D. The maximum time period in which the IRS can collect unpaid taxes.

25. Tax practitioners should use "best practices" when representing a client before the IRS. All of the following are cited as examples of best practices in Circular 230 except:

A. Advising the client regarding any potential accuracy-related penalties.
B. Acting fairly and with integrity in dealings with the IRS.
C. Arriving at a conclusion supported solely by the client's information.
D. Clearly communicating with clients and the IRS.

26. Circular 230 requires practitioners demonstrate _____ when representing their clients.

A. Intelligence
B. Trustworthiness
C. Competence
D. Courtesy

27. Which of the following tax professionals is allowed to practice before the U.S. Tax Court without first passing the Tax Court exam?

A. CPA
B. Attorney
C. Enrolled Actuary
D. Enrolled agent

28. Taxpayers must sign their e-filed 1040 returns:

A. Under penalty of perjury.
B. With an original, handwritten signature.
C. Before the return has been prepared.
D. With a digital signature.

29. Taxpayers often elect the direct deposit option because it is the fastest way of receiving refunds. What is the preparer's responsibility if the taxpayer wishes to direct deposit their refund?

A. A preparer must accept any direct deposit election designated by the taxpayer. The preparer cannot charge an additional fee for direct deposit.
B. A preparer does not have to accept a taxpayer's direct deposit election.
C. A preparer must accept any direct deposit election designated by the taxpayer, but the preparer can charge an additional fee for direct deposit.
D. A preparer does not have to accept any direct deposit election designated by the taxpayer, whether or not an additional fee is charged.

30. Who could be a "responsible person" for purposes of the trust fund recovery penalty?

A. Any person with authority and control over funds to direct their disbursement.
B. Any employee within an organization who has the duty to perform and the power to direct the collecting, accounting, and paying of employment (trust fund) taxes.
C. A member of the board of trustees for a nonprofit charity.
D. All of the above may be a "responsible person."

31. IRC Section 7216 prescribes criminal penalties for tax professionals who illegally:

A. Contact taxpayers by phone or e-mail.
B. Disclose tax return information.
C. Fail to pay taxes due.
D. Fail to file required information returns.

32. In which situation may the IRS contact the taxpayer directly, even if a recognized representative is in place?

A. The taxpayer is outside the United States.
B. The taxpayer has been deemed incompetent.
C. The recognized representative has unreasonably delayed an IRS examination.
D. The recognized representative is not an enrolled tax practitioner.

33. Which of the following types of IRS guidance generally has the highest authority in establishing precedence for all taxpayers?

A. Revenue Ruling.
B. Private letter ruling.
C. Technical advice memoranda.
D. Official IRS publications.

34. Lacey wants to designate her tax preparer, Walcott, as the third-party designee on her individual tax return. Walcott has an AFSP certificate, but no other type of licensing. Based solely on the third-party authorization, which of the following actions will Walcott not be able to take on Lacey's behalf?

A. Walcott can call the IRS for information about the processing of her return.
B. Walcott can speak with the IRS regarding the status of a payment related to Lacey's return.
C. Walcott can respond to IRS notices about math errors on her return.
D. Walcott can receive (but not cash) her tax refund check on her behalf.

35. What is a federal tax lien?

A. A preliminary assessment of tax.
B. A legal seizure of the taxpayer's property to satisfy a tax debt.
C. A legal claim to the property of the taxpayer as security for a tax debt.
D. A collection action by the courts.

36. Yasmin is an enrolled agent who has been in practice for many years. She has just learned that one of her long-time clients, Ronald, is being investigated by the IRS for criminal tax evasion and fraud. What should Yasmin do?

A. End the representation immediately and refer the client to a licensed attorney.
B. Contact the authorities who are investigating her client and offer to turn over all of her client's records.
C. Contact a criminal defense attorney and arrange a deal to jointly represent the client in the criminal proceedings.
D. Enter into discussions with the client in order to prepare a case to defend him against possible criminal charges.

37. Zena is an enrolled agent. She represents Joaquin, whose tax return is under examination by the IRS. Joaquin's tax return was filed jointly with his wife, but they have since divorced. Joaquin does not know the whereabouts of his ex-wife. Joaquin still wants Zena to represent him before the IRS. What is the proper course of action in this case?

A. Zena cannot represent Joaquin during the examination of his previously filed joint return, because she does not have authorization from his ex-wife (who was listed on the return).
B. Zena is allowed to represent Joaquin during the examination of his joint return, but only if he agrees to amend his filing status to married filing separately.
C. Zena is allowed to represent Joaquin during the examination of his joint return, provided Joaquin signs a valid power of attorney (Form 2848).
D. Joaquin must represent himself during the examination of his joint return.

38. Alexander is an enrolled agent. His client, Josefina, asks him the odds of being audited if he claims certain deductions. Alexander replies that the risk is very low, with only 1% of similar tax returns being audited. Is Alexander in violation of Circular 230?

A. Yes. He cannot take into consideration whether a tax return may or may not be audited on a certain issue.
B. No. He is providing good service in helping his client pay the lowest amount of tax.
C. No, but only if the advice he provides is oral and not in writing.
D. Circular 230 does not address this issue.

39. Patsy improperly claims the Earned Income Tax Credit (EITC) on her return. She is later audited. During the audit, Patsy cannot provide documentation to support her EITC claim. The IRS disallows the EITC claim and also imposes interest and penalties. Patsy now has a balance due of over $4,000, including interest and penalties. The IRS later determines that the Social Security number for the dependent claimed on the return was stolen, and Patsy knowingly committed tax fraud. What other possible repercussions are likely for her?

A. The IRS will likely impose a two-year ban on claiming EITC.
B. The IRS will likely impose a ten-year ban on claiming EITC.
C. The IRS will likely impose a lifetime ban on claiming EITC.
D. The IRS will arrest the taxpayer for fraud.

40. Which of the following immediately stops all IRS assessment and collection actions for a taxpayer, regardless of the year and type of assessment?

A. When a taxpayer files in Tax Court.
B. When a taxpayer files for bankruptcy protection.
C. When a taxpayer's authorized representative contacts the IRS on his behalf.
D. When a taxpayer files Form 1127, Extension of Time for Payment Due to Hardship.

41. Benjamin Lopez is an enrolled agent. He wants to print new business cards for his office. Which of the following descriptions would be *prohibited* by Circular 230?

A. Benjamin Lopez, EA, certified to practice before the Internal Revenue Service.
B. Benjamin Lopez, enrolled agent, enrolled to practice before the Internal Revenue Service.
C. Benjamin Lopez, enrolled agent, authorized to practice before the Internal Revenue Service.
D. Benjamin Lopez, EA, enrolled to practice before the IRS.

42. IRS Form 2848 provides space for the information and signatures of up to _____.

A. Two spouses.
B. One tax year.
C. Four authorized representatives.
D. Three different entities.

43. Nellie is an enrolled agent who received a complaint from the Office of Professional Responsibility (OPR). A formal complaint against a practitioner is not required to disclose:

A. The name of the IRS employee who submitted the complaint.
B. The deadline for response to the complaint.
C. The nature of the complaint.
D. The specific sanctions recommended against the practitioner.

44. Bernice is an enrolled agent with a new client, Archer, who owns several rental properties. In reviewing his prior-year tax returns, she discovers that Archer has failed to claim depreciation for any of the rental properties. What should Bernice do in this case to be in compliance with Circular 230 requirements?

A. Insist on amending the client's prior-year tax returns.
B. Promptly advise the client of the error and the consequences of not correcting the error.
C. Contact the IRS, in confidence, to notify revenue agents about the error.
D. Nothing. Claiming depreciation deductions is a choice a taxpayer is free to make, but it is not required.

45. Darden claimed the Earned Income Tax Credit on his most recently-filed tax return. The IRS audited his return and disallowed the EITC in 2022. The IRS also found that Darden claimed the EITC due to reckless disregard of the rules, because he claimed a dependent that was not his qualifying child. For how many tax years is Darden barred from claiming the EITC? Darden cannot claim the EITC for:

A. 1 year.
B. 2 years.
C. 3 years.
D. 4 years.

46. Which of the following disclosures of taxpayer information is not allowed without a taxpayer's written consent?

A. When there is a disclosure of taxpayer information for preparation of state or local tax returns.
B. When a tax preparation firm discloses return information to others in the firm for purposes of assisting in the preparation of the tax return.
C. When a disclosure is made to a taxpayer's fiduciary.
D. When a disclosure solicits business from an existing client, and the business is not related to the IRS.

47. All of the following are examples of disreputable conduct that can lead to suspension or disbarment for an enrolled agent except:

A. Failing to include a valid PTIN on tax returns.
B. Willfully failing to e-file returns electronically if the preparer falls under the e-filing mandate.
C. Solicitation of former clients using direct mail.
D. Maintaining an active partnership with a practitioner who has been disbarred (but does not sign returns).

48. What is the minimum number of continuing education hours that an enrolled agent must take each year of his or her renewal cycle?

A. 16 hours.
B. 18 hours.
C. 24 hours.
D. 72 hours.

49. If an e-filed return is rejected, what is the preparer required to do?

A. The preparer must take reasonable steps to inform the taxpayer within 72 hours of the rejection.
B. The preparer must take reasonable steps to inform the taxpayer within 24 hours of the rejection, with the exception of weekends and holidays.
C. The preparer must take reasonable steps to inform the taxpayer within 24 hours of the rejection.
D. It is the taxpayer's responsibility to ensure that his e-filed return is correctly submitted.

50. Which of the following tasks can be performed by any enrolled agent on behalf of their client?

A. Prepare and file a lawsuit for a refund in the United States District Court.
B. Prepare and sign a protest to challenge examination results in the IRS Appeals Office.
C. Prepare and sign a United States Tax Court petition to contest a notice of deficiency.
D. Prepare and file a bankruptcy petition in a United States Bankruptcy Court due to unpaid tax balances.

51. An enrolled agent is able to represent tax clients before all of the following except:

A. IRS Office of Appeals.
B. IRS Examination division.
C. A U.S. district court.
D. IRS Collections division.

52. Martha is a taxpayer who is unable to pay her tax liability. She applied for an offer in compromise to settle her debt, but the IRS rejected her offer. How many days does Martha have to appeal the rejection?

A. 30 days.
B. 60 days.
C. 90 days.
D. 180 days.

53. Andrea is a tax return preparer. When preparing a return for her client, Darius, Andrea learns that he does not have a bank account to receive a direct deposit of his tax refund. Andrea offers to use her account to receive the direct deposit, and says she will turn the money over to Darius once the refund is deposited. Is this an acceptable action?

A. This is acceptable in all circumstances.
B. This is never acceptable.
C. This is acceptable if Darius signs a power of attorney, giving Andrea the right to receive his refund.
D. This is acceptable if Andrea receives prior written consent from Darius.

54. Chelsea attempted to e-file her tax return on February 15, but her return was rejected because another return bearing her Social Security number had already been filed. She does not know who used her Social Security number. What should Chelsea do?

A. Chelsea must paper-file her return and attach Form 14039, *Identity Theft Affidavit*.
B. Chelsea should attempt to correct the error and e-file the return again.
C. Chelsea should request an identity protection PIN and wait to file her return until she gets it.
D. Chelsea should not file her return if someone has already filed a return using her Social Security number.

55. Disbarred individuals are still allowed to:

A. File powers of attorney with the IRS.
B. State that they are eligible to practice before the IRS.
C. Prepare and submit client-related correspondence with the IRS.
D. Appear before the IRS as a fiduciary or a trustee.

56. In which of the following cases is a power of attorney (Form 2848) not required?

A. When an enrolled agent represents a taxpayer before the IRS appeals division.
B. When a taxpayer wishes to be represented during an IRS examination.
C. By an attorney of record in a case that is docketed in the Tax Court.
D. When a general partner wishes to represent his partnership before the IRS.

57. The IRS will release an existing tax lien in all of the following cases except:

A. When the taxpayer requests an offer in compromise.
B. When the tax debt is fully paid.
C. When the payment of the debt is guaranteed by a bond.
D. When the statute of limitations for collection has expired.

58. All of the following persons may practice before the IRS except:

A. Certified public accountants.
B. Certified financial planners.
C. Enrolled actuaries.
D. Enrolled retirement plan agents.

59. With regard to the Centralized Authorization File (CAF) number on powers of attorney, which of the following statements is true?

A. Powers of attorney that relate to specific tax periods, or to any other Federal tax matter such as application for an employee identification number, will be entered onto the CAF system.
B. A CAF number is an indication of authority to practice before the Internal Revenue Service.
C. The fact that a power of attorney cannot be entered onto the CAF system affects its validity.
D. A power of attorney that does not include a CAF number will not be rejected.

60. Federal law gives the Federal Trade Commission authority to set data safeguard regulations for various entities, including professional tax return preparers. According to the FTC *Safeguards Rule,* tax return preparers are now required to have what type of plan?

A. A written information security plan to protect client data.
B. A well-written engagement letter for each client.
C. A §7216 disclosure consent for each client before starting any engagement.
D. A conflict of interest waiver for each client represented.

61. Jonathan is an enrolled agent who was officially censured by the IRS. What are the consequences after a censure?

A. Jonathan is prohibited from practicing before the IRS.
B. Jonathan is prohibited from filing tax returns.
C. Jonathan is prohibited from practicing before the IRS and from filing tax returns.
D. Jonathan is not prohibited from filing tax returns or representing taxpayers before the IRS.

62. Manuel is an enrolled agent. He sends out a targeted direct mail advertisement to his existing clients once a year. How long must he retain a copy of the advertisement?

A. 36 months from the date of the first mailing or use.
B. 36 months from the date of the last transmission or use.
C. 24 months from the date of the last mailing or use.
D. Four years from the date of the last transmission or use.

63. Celia is an enrolled agent with a client that wishes to take a position regarding a particular tax credit. Celia does some research and discovers that this issue is currently being litigated in the courts, with taxpayers arguing that the Revenue Ruling that the IRS is relying on for this credit does not comply with statutory guidance. The IRS is appealing the issue in several pending cases. It is possible that the issue will continue to be litigated for years. Based on the individual circumstances of her client's case, Celia determines that her client has a good argument for his position. What is Celia's responsibility in this case?

A. Celia cannot sign the return or recommend a position that is contrary to an IRS position.
B. Celia should request a private letter ruling for her client. Otherwise, she may not take the position on the return.
C. Celia can claim the credit on her client's tax return as long as the position is reasonable, is not incorrect, inconsistent, or incomplete; is not frivolous, and is adequately disclosed.
D. Celia can claim the credit on her client's tax return as long as the position is not incorrect, inconsistent, or incomplete and is not frivolous. Additional disclosure is not required.

64. Wallace is an enrolled agent, and Sabrina is his client. Sabrina wants to take a tax position on her return. There is a reasonable basis for the position, based on a recent court case. What is Wallace's duty to his client if he advises Sabrina regarding a position on her tax return, for which penalties may be incurred?

A. Wallace should not advise Sabrina about the possibility of penalties resulting from a tax return that he prepared.
B. Wallace must advise Sabrina of the penalties that are reasonably likely to apply regarding a position on her tax return, if he advises the client regarding the position or if he prepares the tax return.
C. Wallace must advise Sabrina of the possibility of the tax return being audited and estimate the risk of that occurring. If the audit risk is high, he should decline the engagement.
D. Wallace should advise Sabrina of the audit risk, and consider not disclosing the position based on the risk of eventual penalties.

65. Webster just became an enrolled agent. He now wants to apply to become an authorized e-file provider. Which of the following is not a requirement to become an IRS e-file provider?

A. To be a United States citizen or a lawful permanent resident.
B. To be at least 18 years old as of the date of application.
C. To have a permanent business location outside his home, in order to ensure the safety of client confidentiality and client records.
D. To meet applicable state and local licensing or bonding requirements for the preparation and collection of tax returns.

66. Gannon is an enrolled agent. He has a new client this year named Ericka, who has a 5-year-old daughter that she claims as a dependent. Is Gannon required to review the child's birth certificate in order to verify the child's age?

A. Gannon is not required to review the child's birth certificate, unless Gannon has reason to question the child's age.
B. Gannon is required to review the child's birth certificate to verify the child's age and identity.
C. Gannon is required to review and make a copy of the child's birth certificate.
D. Gannon is required to make a copy of the child's birth certificate, as well as to demand a second form of I.D. for the child.

67. A practitioner is required to be in compliance with all existing tax obligations in order to maintain their licensing. Under Circular 230, what is the definition of "tax compliance"?

A. When all returns that are due have been filed.
B. When all returns that are due have been filed, and all taxes that are due have been paid (or acceptable payment arrangements have been established).
C. When all returns that are due have been filed, and all taxes that are due have been paid. A payment arrangement is not sufficient; the taxes must be paid in order to be in compliance.
D. When all taxes that are due have been paid (or acceptable payment arrangements have been established), even if there are unfiled returns.

68. When multiple tax preparers are involved in the preparation of a single return, who is required to sign the return?

A. Any preparer who has the proper licensing may sign the return.
B. Any of the preparers involved in the task of preparation may sign.
C. The signing tax preparer should be the individual preparer who has the primary responsibility for the overall accuracy of the return.
D. Multiple preparers may sign in the preparer section of the return, because all the preparers have joint and several liability for the return's accuracy.

69. Umeko is an enrolled agent. Her client, Kiyoshi, tells her that he used his automobile 100% for business purposes. Kiyoshi does not own any other vehicles. Can Umeko rely on Kiyoshi's statement without any further verification?

A. Yes.
B. No. She needs to verify the information with third parties.
C. No. She must make reasonable inquiries of her client.
D. No. She must review a mileage log and other documents provided by her client before she can claim any deductions.

70. How long must a paid preparer retain a copy of a client's tax return?

A. Three years after the close of the return period.
B. Four years after the close of the return period.
C. Six years after the close of the return period.
D. Indefinitely.

71. Bruno owes $10,000 in federal income tax. He does not dispute the amount but does not have the ability to pay the full amount because he is disabled and cannot work. Bruno agrees to pay $5,000 of his liability as part of an offer in compromise with the IRS based on the grounds of:

A. Doubt as to liability.
B. Undue hardship.
C. Doubt as to collectibility.
D. Effective tax administration.

72. The Electronic Federal Tax Payment System (EFTPS) allows taxpayers and businesses to make federal tax payments electronically. In order to log into the system, which of the following is required?

A. Taxpayer Identification Number (EIN or SSN) and Personal Identification Number (PIN).
B. Taxpayer Identification Number (EIN or SSN) and a password.
C. Taxpayer Identification Number, Personal Identification Number (PIN), and a password.
D. Taxpayer Identification Number (EIN or SSN) and a biometric signature.

73. If a taxpayer does not file their tax return by the due date (including extensions), the taxpayer is most likely to be assessed which of the following penalties?

A. An accuracy-related penalty.
B. A civil fraud penalty.
C. A trust fund recovery penalty.
D. A failure-to-file penalty.

74. All of the following may cause a practitioner to face disciplinary action by the Office of Professional Responsibility except:

A. A misdemeanor conviction for public drunkenness.
B. Misconduct while representing a taxpayer.
C. A felony drug conviction.
D. Giving a false opinion through gross incompetence.

75. When submitting an Offer in Compromise based on "doubt as to collectibility" or "effective tax administration," taxpayers must submit Form 656, *Offer in Compromise*, and also submit:

A. A collection information statement.
B. A lump sum cash offer.
C. Proof of residency.
D. Reasonable offer terms.

76. Desmond is an enrolled agent. During the year, he gets an offer from an investment services firm. The firm wants Desmond to share his client list so the investment firm can market investments to his clients. Desmond agrees, and emails a spreadsheet to the investment firm with all his client's names, addresses and other personal biometric information. Desmond did not ask his clients' permission before sharing this information with the investment firm. What penalty may be assessed against Desmond?

A. No penalty, this type of information disclosure is permitted as long as it is not malicious.
B. Desmond may be assessed an IRC §7216 penalty, for disclosure or use of information by the preparer of the return without the taxpayer's consent.
C. Desmond may be assessed a penalty for criminal fraud under IRC §6663.
D. Desmond may be assessed a due diligence penalty under IRC §6695(g).

77. The key distinction between fraud and negligence is that fraud is always:

A. Intentional.
B. More complex.
C. Harder to detect.
D. More difficult to prosecute.

78. Diego plans to submit Form W-7 for his client, Giovanna, who needs to request an ITIN in order to file her return. What type of identifying documents must accompany the ITIN application?

A. Form W-7 must include photocopies of supporting documentation, such as a passport or birth certificate.
B. Form W-7 must include original or notarized copies of supporting documentation, such as a passport or birth certificate. Photocopies are not sufficient.
C. Form W-7 does not require any additional documentation as long as it is filed with an original return.
D. Form W-7 must include original or certified copies of supporting documentation, such as a passport or birth certificate. Photocopies are no longer sufficient.

79. Mickey fraudulently claimed the American Opportunity Tax Credit. He was not a college student, and did not have any qualifying educational expenses during the year. Mickey received and spent his $2,500 refund when an audit notice was issued. During the examination, Mickey cannot provide documentation to support his AOTC claim. What is likely to happen in this case?

A. The AOTC will be disallowed, and Mickey will have a balance due, including penalties.
B. The AOTC will be disallowed, and Mickey will have a balance due, including penalties and interest. In addition, he may be disallowed from claiming the credit in future years.
C. The credit will be disallowed, but Mickey will not owe any additional penalties.
D. The AOTC will be disallowed for the current year return, but it will not be disallowed in future years.

80. Which of the following practitioners would be allowed to use the term "enrolled agent" to describe their status?

A. A person who has passed all three parts of the EA exam, but who has not received his confirmation of enrollment yet.
B. An enrolled agent who has been placed on inactive status.
C. An enrolled agent who is currently appealing an official OPR censure.
D. An enrolled agent who has let his license lapse.

81. A Refund Anticipation Loan (RAL) is money borrowed by a taxpayer from a lender based on the taxpayer's anticipated income tax refund. Which of the statements below is **correct** regarding RALs?

A. The Internal Revenue Service has active involvement and oversight for Refund Anticipation Loans.
B. The Internal Revenue Service may be liable to the lender for additional interest on a Refund Anticipation Loan.
C. Refund anticipation loans (RALs) are interest-bearing loans made by the Department of the Treasury.
D. The IRS is not involved in the RAL process and is not responsible for Refund Anticipation Loans.

82. During the IRS examination process, a taxpayer has the right to:

A. Request that an enrolled practitioner represents him.
B. Appeal any determination made by the IRS examination division.
C. Decline an IRS summons.
D. Both A and B are correct.

83. Which of the following acts is not considered "practice" before the IRS?

A. Representing a taxpayer before IRS Appeals.
B. Appearing as a witness for a taxpayer.
C. Offering written tax advice with the potential for tax avoidance.
D. Preparing and submitting a response to an IRS notice or inquiry.

84. Landry is an enrolled agent. Which of the following actions would be permitted?

A. Landry uses the official IRS eagle logo in all her advertising.
B. Landry offers to file a client's tax return using the client's last pay stub, instead of Form W-2.
C. Landry offers her clients refund anticipation loans.
D. Landry offers direct deposit of refund checks for a small fee.

85. For the non-refundable $500 "Other Dependent Credit," which of the following would not be a qualifying person for the purposes of the credit?

A. A qualifying relative of the taxpayer, 17 years and older.
B. A qualifying child with ITIN.
C. A qualifying relative, including a taxpayer's aging parent.
D. A qualifying child that is the dependent of another taxpayer.

86. At the end of the year, the following enrolled agents totaled their CE hours for the year. Which of them has not met the minimum annual educational requirements for license renewal?

Preparer	Regular CE	Ethics CE
Sebastian	24 hours	1 hour
Gloria	16 hours	2 hours
Mona	14 hours	4 hours

A. Sebastian
B. Gloria
C. Mona
D. Sebastian and Mona.

87. For the IRS to grant a "guaranteed" installment agreement, a taxpayer must have not failed to file any income tax returns or pay any tax shown on such returns during any of the preceding:

A. 3 taxable years.
B. 5 taxable years.
C. 6 taxable years.
D. 10 taxable years.

88. Which of the following types of documentation is sufficient for a taxpayer to claim a charitable deduction for a cash donation of $250 or more?

A. No documentation is needed for cash donations of under $500.
B. A self-prepared receipt or written acknowledgment is sufficient if the taxpayer also has a canceled check.
C. A receipt or written acknowledgment from the organization listing the date of the donation and the amount contributed, plus a statement from the organization regarding whether the organization gave any goods or services as a result of the contribution.
D. No receipt is required, but the organization must write a good faith estimate of the value of goods and services provided by the organization as a result of the contribution.

89. What is a "30-day letter"?

A. A revenue agent report.
B. A summons to appear before an IRS examiner.
C. A notice explaining a taxpayer's right to appeal and a statement of proposed tax owed after an IRS examination.
D. A notice of deficiency.

90. Circular 230 is found in _____ of the Code of Federal Regulations, which governs practice before the Internal Revenue Service.

A. Title 31
B. Title 26
C. Title 90
D. Title 53

91. Under expedited suspension procedures, the Office of Professional Responsibility can take quicker disciplinary actions against a practitioner who:

A. Has been convicted of a crime involving dishonesty.
B. Has been convicted of a crime involving a breach of trust.
C. Has failed to file his federal income tax returns in four of the five previous tax years.
D. All of the above.

92. If a taxpayer fails to file a return, and the failure is due to *fraud*, the penalty is:

A. 15% for each month or part of a month that the return is late, up to a maximum of 50%.
B. 15% for each month or part of a month that the return is late, up to a maximum of 25%.
C. 10% for each month or part of a month that the return is late, up to a maximum of 50%.
D. 15% for each month or part of a month that the return is late, up to a maximum of 75%.

93. Which of the following actions is <u>permitted</u> by Circular 230?

A. A taxpayer may authorize an enrolled agent to receive a refund check on behalf of the taxpayer.
B. A taxpayer may authorize an enrolled agent to receive and endorse a refund check on behalf of the taxpayer.
C. A taxpayer may authorize an enrolled agent to file their return without a signature.
D. A taxpayer may authorize an enrolled agent to represent them in U.S. district court.

94. What is IRS Direct Pay?

A. Direct Pay is a third-party payment service that charges a fee to withdraw an IRS payment.
B. Direct Pay is a secure IRS service that may be used to pay an individual tax bill or estimated tax payment. The IRS charges a nominal fee for Direct Pay.
C. Direct Pay is an IRS service that may be used by corporations as well as individuals to pay estimated taxes.
D. Direct Pay is a free IRS service that may be used to pay an individual tax bill or estimated tax payment.

95. In any case in which the IRS asserts fraud, what party has the "burden of proof" with respect to the fraud?

A. Taxpayer.
B. Tax preparer.
C. Government.
D. Tax Court.

96. What does the IRS "information matching program" automatically check on each tax return?

A. It looks for typos in the taxpayer's name.
B. It checks for mathematical errors.
C. It scans for errors in the refund amount.
D. It checks against filed information statements to verify that income and major deductions on the return are correct.

97. Which IRS authorization provides the highest degree of representation rights to an enrolled practitioner?

A. Form 2848.
B. Form 8821.
C. Third Party Designee Authorization.
D. Oral Authorization.

98. Warrick has a new client, Selena, who had her prior return prepared with another tax office. Warrick would like to rely on the other practitioner's work product by using the depreciation schedule on the prior-year return. Can he do so without question?

A. Only if the practitioner is another member of the first practitioner's firm.
B. Yes, in all circumstances.
C. No; reliance on another preparer's work product is prohibited.
D. Generally, yes, but due care must be taken if Warrick relies on the work product of another person.

99. Kira is a tax preparer who plans to retire this year. She sells her entire tax practice to Agnes, who is a CPA. With regards to Kira's EFIN, what must occur when a tax business is sold?

A. Agnes is required to submit a new e-file application and request her own EFIN. Kira's EFIN cannot be transferred.
B. Kira may transfer her EFIN to Agnes, as long as the physical location of the practice does not change.
C. Agnes is not required to submit a new e-file application as long as Kira gives her written permission to use the existing one. A formal transfer is not required.
D. The IRS will issue a new EFIN automatically when the preparer's PTIN information changes on the submitted returns.

100. The regulations under Circular 230 governs all of the following persons except:

A. Enrolled agents.
B. CPAs.
C. Licensed insurance broker.
D. Enrolled Actuaries.

Please review your answer choices with the correct answers in the next section.

Answers to Exam #3: Representation

1. The answer is A. A federal tax lien is a document filed with the local recording office that identifies tax liabilities owed by the taxpayer. The lien attaches to all of the taxpayer's property or rights to property. This includes all property, both tangible and intangible property, such as copyrights and patents. The federal tax lien gives the IRS a legal claim to all of the taxpayer's property for the amount of the tax liability.

2. The answer is B. Abella is not considered a paid preparer under Circular 230 rules, so she is not required to obtain a PTIN. If an _employee_ of a business prepares the business' tax returns as part of her job responsibilities, the employee is not required to sign as a paid preparer. Accordingly, unless the employee prepares other federal tax returns for compensation, she would not be required to obtain a PTIN.

3. The answer is C. Judith must write "WITHDRAW" across the top of Form 2848 and send it to the IRS via mail or fax. If an enrolled agent or other practitioner wishes to withdraw from representation of a client, she must write "WITHDRAW" across the top of the first page of Form 2848, Power of Attorney and Declaration of Representative, with his signature and the date below it. It must be either mailed or faxed to the IRS. The form must clearly indicate the applicable tax matters and periods. If a taxpayer decides to revoke a power of attorney, he or she must write "REVOKE" across the top of the form with a signature and the date below it. If neither the taxpayer nor the representative has a copy of the power of attorney, a statement of revocation or withdrawal may be sent to the IRS.

4. The answer is B. Circular 230 §10.37 details expectations for certain types of written advice a practitioner gives a client. When issuing written advice, a practitioner cannot take into consideration the chances that a tax return <u>may or may not be audited</u> or that a particular matter may or may not be raised at audit.

5. The answer is A. Not all enrolled agents are required to pass the EA exam. There are two paths to becoming an enrolled agent. An individual may receive the designation by virtue of past employment with the IRS, rather than by passing the three-part Special Enrollment Examination. An EA candidate must possess a minimum of five years of past service with the IRS that includes technical experience as outlined in Circular 230, which is having been regularly engaged in applying and interpreting Federal tax law. A candidate must apply within three years of leaving the IRS.

6. The answer is C. An EIN is not required to participate in the AFSP program. However, a valid PTIN is mandatory, the participant must consent to be bound by Circular 230, and be subject to a tax compliance check.

7. The answer is C. Under §10.26 of Circular 230, an enrolled practitioner is allowed to be a notary public. However, a notary public who is employed as counsel, attorney, or agent in a matter before the IRS or who has a material interest in the matter cannot engage in any notary activities related to that matter. This includes all enrolled agents and other federally-authorized tax practitioners. In other words, it is fine that Rory is a notary, but he cannot notarize documents for any audit engagement in which he is also representing the taxpayer.

8. The answer is A. If a taxpayer and the IRS fail to settle a non-docketed examination controversy in the IRS Appeals Office, the next event to occur is the issuance of a notice of deficiency, also known as an IRS 90-day letter.

9. The answer is A. The IRS can assess an accuracy-related penalty of 20% of the underpayment of tax against Mandy. This penalty can be asserted for the understatement of income tax because of negligent acts or a disregard of the rules or regulations. "Negligent acts" include the failure to keep adequate books and records (based on a released EA exam question).

10. The answer is D. The practice of enrolled actuaries is limited to certain Internal Revenue Code sections that relate to their area of expertise, principally those sections governing employee retirement plans.

11. The answer is A. Under IRC section 7525, communications relating to tax advice between an enrolled agent and a taxpayer are confidential to the same extent that the communications would be privileged if they were between a taxpayer and an attorney, and the advice relates to:

- Noncriminal tax matters before the IRS, or
- Noncriminal tax proceedings brought in federal court by or against the United States.

This confidentiality privilege does *not* extend to:

- Communications regarding tax shelters.
- Communications in furtherance of a crime or fraud.
- Any criminal matter before the IRS.
- The preparation of tax returns.

12. The answer is B. The IRS provides a "transmission perfection period" for rejected returns. Individual returns are given a 5-day perfection period, while most business returns are given a 10-day perfection period. Note that the "transmission perfection period" is not an extension of time to file; it is merely an allowed period to correct errors in a previously submitted e-file.

13. The answer is B. If an individual loses eligibility to practice, the IRS will not recognize a power of attorney that names the individual as a representative. Individuals who have been disbarred as a result of certain actions cannot practice before the IRS.

14. The answer is D. Both taxpayers are "jointly and severally" liable for the tax and penalties on a joint return even if they later divorce. "Joint and several liability" means that each taxpayer is legally responsible for the entire liability. Thus, both spouses are generally held responsible for all the tax due, even if one spouse earned all the income or claimed improper deductions or credits. This is also true even if a divorce decree states that a former spouse will be responsible for any amounts due on previously filed joint returns.

15. The answer is C. Under Circular 230, preparers are required to keep copies of all returns they have prepared **or** to retain a list of clients and tax returns prepared. At a minimum, the list must contain the taxpayer's name and taxpayer identification number, the tax year, and the type of return prepared. The copies or the list may be stored either electronically or as hard copies. The copies of tax returns or the lists must be retained for at least three years after the close of the return period.

16. The answer is A. A licensed tax attorney would be an example of an ERO. Certified Network Administrators maintain computer networks. They are not Electronic Return Originators (ERO). Neither human resource specialists nor volunteer retirement coordinators would be considered an ERO.

17. The answer is C. Failure to timely file tax returns or to pay income taxes may be grounds for denying an application for enrollment. The Return Preparer Office will review all of the facts and circumstances to determine whether a denial of enrollment is warranted. Answer A is incorrect because an enrolled agent is not required to have a Social Security number. Answer B is incorrect because U.S. citizenship is not required to practice before the IRS. Answer D is incorrect because insolvency and bankruptcy are not grounds to deny enrollment.

18. The answer is D. Although the credit is refundable, Form 8867 is not required for the Credit for Excess Social Security and RRTA Tax Withheld. In previous years, the law required paid preparers to complete and submit Form 8867 with every EITC claim. Form 8867 now includes the Child Tax Credit (CTC) and the Additional Child Tax Credit (ACTC), the American Opportunity Tax Credit (AOTC), the Credit for Other Dependents (ODC), and the Head of Household (HOH) filing status. Paid preparers are now required to submit Form 8867 with every electronic or paper return claiming EITC, CTC, and/or ACTC, AOTC, ODC, and HOH filing status.

19. The answer is A. Generally, when a taxpayer files bankruptcy, the 10-year collection statute is suspended by the length of time the taxpayer is in bankruptcy, plus an additional six months (IRC section 6503(h)(2) and IRM, Part 5, *Collecting Process*).

20. The answer is D. Only U.S. citizens and legal U.S. resident aliens with a valid SSN can claim EITC. In addition, the SSN must be valid for work purposes. A taxpayer cannot claim EITC using an Individual Taxpayer Identification Number (ITIN) or Adoption Taxpayer Identification Number (ATIN).

21. The answer is B. Reginald can seek reinstatement from the Office of Professional Responsibility five years after disbarment. Reinstatement is not guaranteed and will not be granted unless the Internal Revenue Service is satisfied that the practitioner is not likely to engage in conduct contrary to IRS regulations, and that granting such reinstatement would not be contrary to the public interest.

22. The answer is A. Esther must respond to the summons. A summons legally compels a person, taxpayer, or third party to meet with the IRS and provide information, documents, or testimony. An individual has the right to contest a summons based on various technical, procedural, or constitutional grounds. However, if a taxpayer or other witness fails to respond to a summons within the prescribed period, the IRS may seek judicial enforcement through U.S. district court.

23. The answer is B. Once a tax liability is <u>assessed</u>, the statute of limitations for collection begins to run. In general, the date of assessment is the date on which the IRS receives a taxpayer's return with a tax owed. If a taxpayer does not file a return, the assessment date is the date on which the IRS assesses any additional tax owed. There is no statute of limitations for instances where a return is not filed, or a fraudulent return was filed.

24. The answer is A. The assessment statute of limitations refers to the period in which the IRS can assess a tax deficiency for a certain year. Generally, the statute of limitations for the IRS to assess a deficiency expires three years from the due date of the return or the date on which the return was filed, whichever is later. There is an extended statute in cases of substantial omission of income and fraud.

25. The answer is C. "Best practices," according to Circular 230, include:

- Clearly communicating with a client regarding the terms of engagement.
- Establishing relevant facts, evaluating the reasonableness of assumptions or representations, relating the applicable law to the relevant facts, and arriving at a conclusion supported by the law and the facts (*not* just by the client's information, as stated in the incorrect answer choice).
- Advising the client regarding any potential penalties.
- Acting fairly and with integrity while practicing before the IRS.

26. The answer is C. Section 10.35 of Circular 230 states that a practitioner must be *"competent to engage in practice"* before the IRS. Competence is defined as having the appropriate level of knowledge, skill, thoroughness, and preparation for the specific matter or matters related to a client's engagement. In accordance with Circular 230, a practitioner can become competent in various ways, including consulting with experts in the relevant area or studying the relevant law. Section 10.35 replaces the complex rules that previously governed covered opinions.

27. The answer is B. Only licensed attorneys are allowed to practice before the U.S. Tax Court without passing a qualifying test. EAs and CPAs must take a separate exam that gives them the right to practice before the Tax Court. The U.S. Tax Court Exam is intended for applicants who are not attorneys; only by passing this exam may a non-attorney practice before the U.S. Tax Court.

28. The answer is A. Taxpayers must sign their returns under penalty of perjury. This means that the taxpayer must make a declaration that the return is true, correct, and complete to the best of the knowledge and belief of the taxpayer. Answer "B" is incorrect because an original handwritten signature is not required if the taxpayer is signing using one of the acceptable electronic methods, which is available if the return is e-filed. Answer "C" is incorrect because returns must be signed by the taxpayer after the return is complete. Answer "D" is incorrect because there are many acceptable methods of signing an e-filed tax return, including electronic signatures and handwritten signatures.

29. The answer is A. A preparer must accept any direct deposit election to any eligible financial institution designated by the taxpayer. Preparers cannot charge an additional fee for this service.

30. The answer is D. The trust fund recovery penalty (TFRP) may be assessed against any person who is responsible for collecting or paying income and employment taxes withheld, and who willfully fails to pay them. A responsible person is any person who has the duty to perform and the power to direct the collecting, accounting, and paying of trust fund taxes. This person may be:

- An officer or an employee of a corporation.
- A member or employee of a partnership.
- A corporate director or shareholder.
- A member of a board of trustees of a nonprofit organization.
- Another person with authority and control over funds to direct their disbursement.
- Another corporation or third-party payer.

31. The answer is B. IRC Section Internal Revenue Code Sec. 7216 is a *criminal* provision that prohibits preparers of tax returns from knowingly or recklessly disclosing or using tax return information. A convicted preparer may be fined or imprisoned up to one year (or both) for each violation. Civil penalties may also apply.

32. The answer is C. When a recognized representative has unreasonably delayed or hindered an examination, collection, or investigation, an Internal Revenue Service employee may request the permission of his immediate supervisor to contact the taxpayer directly for information. Answer "D" is incorrect because a representative does not necessarily have to be an enrolled practitioner for his power of attorney to be valid (for example, a father who is representing a son or an executor representing an estate).

33. The answer is A. Revenue rulings are written determinations released by the IRS that interpret the tax laws as applied to specific factual situations. Answer "B" is incorrect, because a private letter ruling applies only to the individual taxpayer who requests the ruling. Answer "C" is incorrect because technical advice memoranda (TAM) provides non-binding written advice in response to questions that arise from examinations. Answer "D" is incorrect because IRS publications are not substantial authority. They are advisory only and have no binding effect on the IRS.

34. The answer is D. Walcott <u>cannot</u> receive Lacey's refund check. A third-party authorization is not sufficient to designate a preparer to receive a tax refund check; plus, Walcott is not able to receive a taxpayer's refund check, because he is not an enrolled agent, CPA, or attorney. A signed Form 2848, Power of Attorney and Declaration of Representative, must be used in order for a tax professional to receive a client's refund check. Form 2848 is also used to authorize an individual to represent a taxpayer or an entity before the IRS. A third-party authorization automatically ends one year from the due date of the return.

35. The answer is C. A federal tax lien is a legal claim to the property of the taxpayer as security for a tax debt. Generally, a federal tax lien will continue until the liability is satisfied, it becomes unenforceable by lapse of time (the collection statute expires), or a bond is accepted in the amount of the liability.

36. The answer is A. Yasmin should end the representation immediately and refer the client to a licensed attorney. If a practitioner becomes aware that a client is being investigated for criminal fraud, the preparer should end representation. Generally, only criminal tax attorneys would have the appropriate legal expertise needed in such cases. In addition, a tax preparer may be considered a witness in the criminal investigation, since section 7525 practitioner-client confidentiality privilege does not cover criminal matters. Communications in the context of a civil proceeding that later becomes a criminal case are likewise not covered.

37. The answer is C. Zena is allowed to represent Joaquin during the examination of his joint return, provided Joaquin signs a valid power of attorney (Form 2848). In the case of a joint return, both taxpayers may decide independently whether or not they want to be represented by a recognized representative (either by the same representative or by different representatives), or not represented at all. Each spouse must execute their own separate Form 2848 if they want to be represented.

38. The answer is A. Yes, Alexander is in violation of Circular 230. He cannot take into consideration the chances that his client's tax return may or may not be audited, or that a particular matter may or may not be raised on audit. Alexander is playing "audit lottery," which is a type of practitioner advice that is specifically prohibited by the IRS in Circular 230.

39. The answer is B. The IRS will likely impose a ten-year ban on Patsy from claiming EITC (if there is evidence of fraud). If the error is because of "reckless or intentional disregard" of the rules (but not fraud), the IRS could ban the taxpayer from claiming EITC for the next two years. The IRS cannot impose a lifetime ban on a taxpayer. These bans also apply to the AOTC and Child Tax Credit/Additional Child Tax Credit.

40. The answer is B. There is an automatic stay of all IRS assessment and collection of tax when a taxpayer files for bankruptcy protection. The stay remains in effect until the bankruptcy court lifts it or discharges liabilities, meaning they are eliminated or no longer legally enforceable.

41. The answer is A. Enrolled agents cannot use the term "certified" when describing their professional designation. The other choices would be allowable.

42. The answer is C. Form 2848 provides space for the information and signatures of up to four authorized representatives. If the taxpayer wants to authorize more than four representatives, the taxpayer must write "See attached for additional representatives," in the space to the right of line 2 of Form 2848 and attach an additional Form(s) 2848 for the additional authorized representatives.

43. The answer is A. An official complaint against a practitioner from the OPR is not required to disclose the name or identity of the employee who submitted the complaint. The complaint must include the nature of the complaint, a demand for an answer to the charges, instructions on how to respond to the complaint, the specific charges against the practitioner, and the sanctions recommended.

44. The answer is B. Bernice must promptly advise her client of the error and the consequences of not correcting the error. Under section 10.21 of Circular 230, a practitioner is required to promptly notify a client of an error or omission and advise him of the consequences of not correcting the error or omission. A practitioner, however, is not required to amend prior year returns, nor is she required to notify the IRS about a client's errors.

45. The answer is B. Darden will not be allowed to claim the credit for at least two tax years. There are special restrictions on EITC claims by taxpayers who have had previous EITC claims denied. A taxpayer who claimed the EITC due to reckless or intentional disregard of the EITC rules cannot claim the EITC for two tax years. If the error was due to fraud, the taxpayer cannot claim the EITC for ten tax years.

46. The answer is D. A tax preparer cannot make disclosures to solicit additional business from an existing client for business unrelated to the IRS (for example, disclosures to sell or solicit insurance, stocks, or other financial services). In this case, the preparer would need written consent from the client.

47. The answer is C. Solicitation by mail of a former client is not disreputable conduct. It is disallowed only if the client or former client has communicated that he does not want to be solicited. The OPR can censure, suspend, or disbar a practitioner from practice before the IRS for incompetence or for disreputable conduct, such as giving false or misleading information, or participating in any business, or accepting assistance from a disbarred practitioner. Disreputable conduct also includes:

- Willfully failing to e-file returns electronically when subject to the e-filing mandate, and
- Failing to include a valid PTIN on tax returns.

48. The answer is A. An enrolled agent is required to complete a minimum of 16 hours of continuing education each year. Two of these hours must be an IRS-approved ethics course. Enrolled agents must always use an IRS-approved CE provider.

49. The answer is C. The preparer must take reasonable steps to inform the taxpayer within 24 hours of the rejection. This is regardless of any holidays, weekends, etc. The 24-hour deadline is a hard deadline. In addition, the preparer is required to disclose the reasons for rejection.

50. The answer is B. An enrolled agent may prepare and sign a protest to challenge examination results in the IRS Appeals Office.

51. The answer is C. An enrolled agent's practice rights do not extend to representation before the U.S. courts—except for the United States Tax Court—and *only* if they pass a special U.S. Tax Court exam and meet other U.S. Tax Court practice requirements. An enrolled agent cannot represent a client in U.S. district court unless he or she is also a licensed attorney.

52. The answer is A. Martha must appeal a rejected offer in compromise within 30 days. Submitting an offer in compromise does not ensure that the IRS will accept the offer. In fact, OIC applications are frequently rejected.

53. The answer is B. Direct deposit of a taxpayer's refund can be designated only to an account in the taxpayer's name. It would be both illegal and unethical for Andrea to specify her own bank account as the designated account to receive a taxpayer's refund.

54. The answer is A. Chelsea must file her tax return on paper, and attach Form 14039, *Identity Theft Affidavit,* to her return. Answer "B" is incorrect, because once a taxpayer's Social Security number has been used on a return, another return cannot be e-filed in the same tax year. Answer "C" is incorrect, because once a taxpayer has already been a victim of Stolen Identity Refund Fraud (SIRF), then obtaining an IP PIN will not help. The IP PIN must be obtained in advance. Chelsea could request an IP PIN for future tax years, but in the current year, she has no choice but to send the return in on paper. Answer "D" is incorrect, because Chelsea is still required to file a correct return, even if she is a victim of refund fraud.

55. The answer is D. Disbarred individuals are prohibited from practice before the IRS. However, a disbarred individual is still allowed to perform duties in certain capacities before the IRS. A suspended or disbarred individual may:

- Represent himself with respect to any matter.
- Appear before the IRS as a trustee, receiver, guardian, administrator, executor, or other fiduciary if duly authorized under the law of the relevant jurisdiction.
- Appear as a witness for the taxpayer.
- Furnish information at the request of the IRS or any of its officers.
- Receive information concerning a taxpayer from the IRS pursuant to a valid tax information authorization.

56. The answer is C. A power of attorney is not required to be submitted by an attorney of record in a case that is docketed in the Tax Court. The U.S. Tax Court has its own rules of practice and procedure and its own rules regarding admission to practice before it. Accordingly, the rules of practice in Circular 230 differ from the rules of practice for the Tax Court.

57. The answer is A. A request for an offer in compromise will not release a tax lien. The IRS will release a lien:

- When the tax debt is fully paid.
- When payment of the debt is guaranteed by a bond.
- When the statute period for collection has ended (in this case, the release is automatic).

58. The answer is B. Certified financial planners are not classified as "enrolled practitioners" under Circular 230 and cannot practice before the IRS. Enrolled practitioners include: enrolled agents, enrolled retirement plan agents, certified public accountants, and licensed attorneys.

59. The answer is D. A power of attorney that does not include a CAF number will not be rejected. If a new preparer or new representative submits a power of attorney and the CAF number is blank, a new CAF number will generally be assigned. The CAF number is a unique nine-digit identification number that the IRS assigns to representatives. Answer "B" is incorrect, because a CAF number is not an indication of authority to practice. Answer "A" is incorrect because there are certain tax matters that will not be entered into the CAF system, but the power of attorney will still be valid for those matters. Answer "C" is incorrect because a power of attorney that cannot be entered into the CAF system can still be a valid power of attorney.

60. The answer is A. Tax preparers are now required by law to have a written information security plan to protect their clients' data (see Publication 4457, *Safeguarding Taxpayer Data*). Answer "B" is incorrect, because the IRS does not mandate the use of engagement letters. Answer "C" is incorrect because a §7216 disclosure consent would only be required for a situation where the preparer had to disclose client information. Answer "D" is incorrect because a conflict of interest waiver is not required unless there is an actual conflict of interest.

61. The answer is D. Jonathan is not prohibited from filing tax returns or representing taxpayers before the IRS. A censure is a public reprimand, with the practitioner's name published in the Internal Revenue Bulletin. The facts of the case that triggered the censure are not published. Unlike disbarment or suspension, censure generally does not prevent a practitioner from filing tax returns or representing taxpayers before the IRS. However, in certain situations, a censure may place conditions on a practitioner's future representations in order to promote high standards of conduct.

62. The answer is B. Targeted direct mail solicitations are permitted under Circular 230. Manuel must retain a copy of all solicitations for a period of at least 36 months from the date of the last transmission or use.

63. The answer is C. Celia can recommend or advise a client on a position, as long as the position is reasonable and not incorrect, inconsistent, or incomplete; and is not frivolous. If the position taken runs contrary to currently stated tax law, the position taken must be adequately disclosed on the return to avoid potential penalties. Celia may use Form 8275, *Disclosure Statement,* to disclose a position on the tax return that runs contrary to the current Revenue Ruling.

64. The answer is B. Wallace must advise Sabrina of the penalties that are reasonably likely to apply regarding a position on her tax return, if he advises her regarding the position or if he prepares the tax return. Under Circular 230 section 10.34, a practitioner must advise the client of the penalties that are reasonably likely to apply regarding a position on a tax return, if Wallace advised Sabrina regarding the position or if he prepared the tax return. Wallace must also advise the client of how to avoid these penalties through disclosure (or by not taking the position). However, the practitioner is prohibited from taking into consideration the chances that a tax return may or may not be audited, or that a particular matter may or may not be raised on audit.

65. The answer is C. Webster is not required to have a permanent business location outside his home. Many e-file providers work exclusively from home offices. An authorized IRS e-file provider is a business authorized by the IRS to participate in IRS e-file. The business may be a sole proprietorship, partnership, or corporation. The provider applicant must:

- Be a United States citizen or a legal U.S. alien lawfully admitted for permanent residence,
- Be at least 18 years old as of the date of application, and
- Meet applicable state and local licensing and/or bonding requirements for the preparation and collection of tax returns.

66. The answer is A. Gannon is not required to review the child's birth certificate to verify the child's age. But, if Gannon has reason to question the child's age, he must investigate further, which may mean requesting the birth certificate. See the IRS page on *Due Diligence FAQ* for more information.

67. The answer is B. A preparer is in compliance if all tax returns that are due have been filed and all taxes that are due have been paid (or acceptable payment arrangements have been established).

68. The answer is C. The signing preparer should be the preparer who has <u>primary responsibility</u> for the accuracy of the return (Treasury Regulations 1.6695-1(b) and 301.7701-15(b)(1)). The requirement that all preparers obtain a PTIN did not change the rules regarding who should be the signing tax return preparer.

69. The answer is C. Although Umeko may rely in good faith, without independent verification, on information furnished by her client, Umeko would not be exercising due diligence under section 10.22 of Circular 230 if she accepted such a statement from her client without further information. In such a situation, the OPR says a practitioner must make *reasonable inquiries* of the client, including, for example, the following:

- Does the client have another automobile for personal use?
- Did the client commute to work?
- Did the client keep records of the business mileage?

70. The answer is A. Tax preparers are required to retain a complete copy of each return they have prepared, or a list of taxpayers' names and TINs, and the tax years for which returns were prepared. The copies or list must be retained for a minimum of three years after the close of the return period (or three years after filing the return, if later. For example, in the case of a delinquent return, the practitioner should retain a copy three years after the return is actually filed).

71. The answer is C. The IRS may accept an offer in compromise from Bruno based on "doubt as to collectibility." There is no dispute that he owes the tax, but it is doubtful that he could ever pay the full amount of tax liability owed within the remainder of the statutory period for collection.

72. The answer is C. EFTPS is a secure IRS website that allows businesses and individuals to make federal tax payments electronically. To log into EFTPS, an enrolled user must be authenticated with three pieces of unique information:

- Taxpayer Identification Number (EIN or SSN),
- EFTPS Personal Identification Number (PIN) and
- an Internet password.

73. The answer is D. If a taxpayer does not file their tax return by the due date (including extensions), the taxpayer may have to pay a failure-to-file penalty. The penalty is 5% of the unpaid balance for each month or part of a month that the return is late, but not more than 25%.

74. The answer is A. A misdemeanor conviction alone is unlikely to cause a practitioner to face disciplinary action from the OPR. There are four broad categories of preparer misconduct, all of which may result in disciplinary action:

- Misconduct while representing a taxpayer.
- Misconduct related to the practitioner's own return.
- Giving a false opinion, knowingly, recklessly, or through gross incompetence.
- Misconduct not directly involving IRS representation, such as a felony conviction.

75. The answer is A. When submitting an Offer in Compromise (OIC) based on "doubt as to collectibility" or "effective tax administration," taxpayers must submit *Form 656, Offer in Compromise,* and also submit a collection information statement. Form 433-A is required for individuals, and Form 433-B is required for businesses.[7]

76. The answer is B. Desmond would likely be assessed a §7216 penalty, which applies to the disclosure or use of information by the preparer without the taxpayer's consent. Tax preparers are not permitted to share a taxpayer's personal biometric information with third parties without the taxpayer's prior written consent. Upon conviction, the §7216 penalty can be up to $1,000 per infraction and/or up to one year in prison, plus the costs of prosecution. The penalty increases to $100,000 if in connection with identity theft.

77. The answer is A. Fraud, as distinguished from negligence, is always *intentional*. One of the elements of fraud is the intent to evade tax. Some badges of fraud that the IRS looks for include:

- False explanations regarding understated or omitted income.
- Large discrepancies between actual and reported deductions from income.
- Concealment of income sources.
- Hiding or transferring assets or income
- Numerous errors in the taxpayer's favor.
- Fictitious records or other deceptions.
- Large omissions of personal service income, specific items of income, gambling winnings, or illegal income.
- False deductions, exemptions, or credits.
- Failure to keep or furnish records.
- Incomplete information given to the return preparer regarding a fraudulent scheme.
- Large and/or frequent cash dealings that may or may not be common to the taxpayer's business.
- Verbal misrepresentations of the facts and circumstances.

Generally, the presence of only one indication of fraud is not sufficient to determine fraud has actually taken place (i.e., unreported income *alone* does not necessarily prove fraud).

---

[7] Any OIC applications received are now returned without consideration if taxpayers haven't filed all required tax returns. The application fee is returned, and any required initial payment submitted with the OIC is applied to outstanding tax debt.

78. The answer is D. Forms W-7, *Application for IRS Individual Taxpayer Identification Number,* must include original or certified copies of documentation such as passports and birth certificates. Notarized copies of documentation are no longer accepted.

> **Note:** Another option is for the taxpayer to use a CAA, or Certified Acceptance Agent to validate their documents. Once the CAA reviews and certifies the taxpayer's original documents, the taxpayer can keep them. The CAA will submit copies of the documents, along with the ITIN application. Tax practitioners can apply to the CAA program by taking the required certification courses and applying to participate in the IRS acceptance agent program.

79. The answer is B. The AOTC will be disallowed, and Mickey will have a balance due, including penalties and interest. In addition, he may be disallowed from claiming the credit in future years. The PATH Act extended the same due diligence requirements for the Earned Income Tax Credit, to the Child Tax Credit, and the American Opportunity Tax Credit. The due diligence requirements also apply to the determination of head of household filing status.

80. The answer is C. An enrolled agent who is appealing an official censure may still use the designation of enrolled agent, as long as he is not disbarred, suspended, or placed on inactive status. A person who has passed the exam but has not completed the application process may not use the designation of enrolled agent to describe his status. An enrolled agent who is on inactive status or who has not renewed his license may not use the designation.

81. The answer is D. Refund anticipation loans (RALs) are interest-bearing loans made by banks, facilitated by tax preparers and tax preparer software, that allow taxpayers to receive an advance on their tax refund from the IRS.[8] A RAL is a loan designed to give taxpayers their income tax refund more quickly for a fee. The taxpayer's refund is then paid directly to the loan originator as payment on the loan. The IRS is not involved in this contract between the taxpayer and a lender, and the IRS cannot grant or deny the RAL. RALs are repaid directly to the lender, typically within 5 to 14 days. (question modified from a released EA exam question).

82. The answer is D. Taxpayers have a right to be represented during the examination process. They also have a right to appeal if they disagree with the examination report. However, taxpayers do not have a right to ignore or decline an IRS summons, although they can request representation during the summons process.

83. The answer is B. Merely appearing as a witness for a taxpayer is not considered "practice before the IRS." Practice before the IRS includes all matters connected with a presentation to the service or to any of its officers or employees relating to a client's rights, responding to official IRS notices, and offering written tax advice with the potential for tax avoidance.

---

[8] See TIGTA report: Characteristics of Users of Refund Anticipation Loans and Refund Anticipation Checks.

84. The answer is C. Landry may offer financial products, including refund anticipation loans. None of the other actions listed would be permitted. Answer "A" is incorrect, because practitioners may not use the IRS eagle logo in their advertising. Answer "B" is incorrect, because e-file providers are prohibited from submitting returns to the IRS prior to the receipt of all Forms W-2, W-2G, and 1099-R from the taxpayer, (they cannot use the taxpayer's last pay stub in lieu of a Form W-2). Answer "D" is incorrect because tax preparers cannot charge a fee for direct deposit.

85. The answer is D. A child that is the qualifying child of another taxpayer would not be a qualifying person for the non-refundable "Other Dependent Credit."

86. The answer is A. The ethics requirement for the enrolled agent license renewal is a minimum of two hours of ethics per year, so Sebastian has not fulfilled his ethics requirement. Circular 230 specifies a minimum of 16 hours of continuing education credit per year, with at least two hours devoted to ethics. If a preparer takes more than two hours of ethics in a single year, the extra ethics hours can count toward the overall minimum requirement for the enrollment cycle, which means that Mona has met her annual CE requirement by virtue of the additional ethics hours she has taken.

87. The answer is B. For the IRS to grant a "guaranteed" installment agreement, a taxpayer must have not failed to file any income tax returns or pay any tax shown on such returns during the preceding five years (question based on a released EA exam question).

88. The answer is C. For cash donations of $250 or more, the taxpayer must have a receipt or written acknowledgment from the charitable organization that includes:

- The amount of cash the taxpayer contributed.
- The date of the contribution.
- Whether the qualified organization gave any goods or services as a result of the contribution.
- If applicable, a description and a good faith estimate of the value of goods or services provided by the organization as a result of the contribution.

As part of their due diligence, tax preparers should ask their clients about the type of substantiation they have for charitable contributions. A taxpayer is expected to be able to substantiate any item on his tax return. A taxpayer cannot deduct amounts that are estimates.

89. The answer is C. After a taxpayer has a closing conference with an IRS examiner, he will receive a "30-day letter." This letter includes a notice explaining the taxpayer's right to appeal the proposed changes; a copy of the revenue agent report that explains the examiner's proposed changes; an agreement or waiver form; and a copy of Publication 5, Your Appeals Rights and How to Prepare a Protest If You Don't Agree. The notice is known as the 30-day letter because the taxpayer has 30 days from the date of the notice to accept or appeal the proposed changes.

90. The answer is A. Circular 230, which is found in Title 31 of the Code of Federal Regulations, governs practice before the Internal Revenue Service. For reference, the Internal Revenue Code is found in Title 26 of the U.S. Code.

91. The answer is D. Under Circular 230 section 10.82; the OPR may move quickly to sanction practitioners by using expedited procedures in certain circumstances, including when a practitioner has been convicted of a crime involving dishonesty or breach of trust. The procedures are also allowed when a practitioner has demonstrated a pattern of "willful disreputable conduct" involving the following:

- Failing to file his federal income tax returns in four of the five previous tax years.
- Failing to file a return required more frequently than annually (such as an employment tax return) during five of the seven previous tax periods.
- In addition, the expedited suspension procedures are allowed when an attorney or CPA has already had his license revoked for cause by any state licensing agency or board.

92. The answer is D. If a taxpayer fails to file a return, and the failure to file is due to *fraud*, the penalty is 15% for each month or part of a month that the return is late, up to a maximum of 75% of the taxpayer's underpayment. This penalty will be *added* to the amount of tax, interest, and penalties that the taxpayer already owes.

93. The answer is A. As described in the instructions to Form 2848, a taxpayer may authorize an attorney, CPA or enrolled agent to receive a refund check on behalf of the taxpayer. However, a tax practitioner may not, under any circumstances, endorse (or cash) a taxpayer's refund check. Answer "C" and "D" are incorrect because an enrolled agent cannot file a return without a valid signature, and an enrolled agent cannot represent a taxpayer in district court.

94. The answer is D. Direct Pay is a secure IRS service that allows individual taxpayers to pay their estimated taxes or individual tax bill online. Direct Pay cannot be used by business taxpayers (such as corporations); it is for individuals only. If a corporation is required to pay federal income tax, the corporation is required to use EFTPS; it cannot use Direct Pay.

95. The answer is C. In cases involving fraud, the burden of proof rests with the government. In a typical proceeding in the United States Tax Court, the taxpayer generally has the burden to prove their position by a preponderance of the evidence. The taxpayer's explanations, or lack of explanations, may help distinguish between civil and criminal fraud. A criminal conviction for tax evasion (under section 7201) establishes liability for the civil fraud penalty. The civil fraud penalty can be imposed even when the taxpayer is acquitted in a criminal fraud prosecution. However, when it comes to an examination of a taxpayer's return, the taxpayer has the burden of proof to substantiate expenses in order to deduct them. A taxpayer can usually meet this burden of proof by having receipts for the expenses.

96. The answer is D. The IRS "information matching program" automatically checks each tax return for accuracy, using filed information statements to verify that income and major deductions on the return are correct. For example, the IRS uses previously reported Forms W-2 and Forms 1099 information that is reported on the taxpayer's return. With these information-matching programs, the IRS detects inconsistencies between third-party information statements and taxpayer data. If an error is detected, the taxpayer receives an IRS notice.

97. The answer is A. Form 2848 is a power of attorney form that is a taxpayer's written authorization for an eligible individual to act on the taxpayer's behalf in tax matters. Any enrolled practitioner (generally, enrolled agents, CPAs, and tax attorneys) can be designated as a representative on Form 2848 and can receive confidential tax information and perform other actions specified on the form, such as representing a taxpayer at an IRS appeals conference. In contrast, Form 8821, *Tax Information Authorization,* does not confer any representation rights. It simply authorizes an individual, corporation, firm, organization, or partnership to inspect or receive confidential information for the type of tax and periods listed. The Third-Party Designee Authorization also does not confer representation rights, either. An oral authorization is used in limited circumstances when a taxpayer wishes to involve a third party in a telephone conversation with the IRS. It is limited to the conversation in which the taxpayer provides the authorization. An oral authorization is automatically revoked once the conversation has ended.

98. The answer is D. Warrick may generally rely on the work product of another practitioner. Circular 230 allows a practitioner to rely on the work product (or the advice) of another practitioner, as long as the practitioner exercises due diligence and "reasonable care." In the case of tax advice, the advice must be reasonable, and the reliance must be in good faith. However, a practitioner cannot rely on another practitioner's work product or advice if he knows (or reasonably should know) that:

- The advice or work product is not reliable, or has obvious errors.
- The person giving the advice is not competent or qualified. For instance, if the practitioner giving the advice has limited knowledge of tax law, he would not be competent.
- The person giving the advice has a conflict of interest that violates Circular 230.

99. The answer is A. Agnes is required to submit an e-file application and request a new EFIN. Kira's EFIN cannot be transferred to Agnes. Preparers who acquire an existing IRS e-file business by purchase, transfer, or gift must submit a new IRS e-file application and receive a new electronic filing identification number (EFIN).

100. The answer is C. Licensed insurance brokers are not enrolled practitioners, and are not regulated by Circular 230. However, if a licensed insurance broker prepares tax returns for compensation, they can be liable for preparer penalties just like any other paid tax practitioner.

This page intentionally left blank.

About the Authors

Joel Busch, CPA, JD

Joel Busch is a tax professor at San Jose State University, where he teaches courses at both the graduate and undergraduate levels. Previously, he was in charge of tax audits, research, and planning for one of the largest civil construction and mining companies in the United States. He received both a BS in Accounting and an MS in Taxation from SJSU, and he has a JD from the Monterey College of Law. He is licensed in California as both a CPA and an attorney.

Christy Pinheiro, EA, ABA®

Christy Pinheiro is an Enrolled Agent and an Accredited Business Accountant. Christy was an accountant for two private CPA firms and for the State of California before going into private practice.

Thomas A. Gorczynski, EA, USTCP

Thomas A. Gorczynski is an Enrolled Agent, a Certified Tax Planner, and admitted to the bar of the United States Tax Court. Tom is also a nationally known tax educator and currently serves as editor-in-chief of EA Journal. He received the 2019 Excellence in Education Award from the National Association of Enrolled Agents. He earned a Master of Science in Taxation from Golden Gate University and a Certificate in Finance and Accounting from the Wharton School at the University of Pennsylvania.

See more information on our official website: *www.PassKeyOnline.com.*

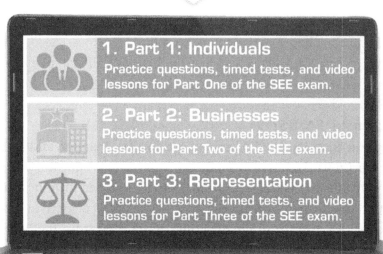

Made in the USA
Las Vegas, NV
10 February 2024